Graphic

Breaking into Design

Graphic

Breaking into Graphic Design

Tips from the Pros on Finding the Right Position for You

Michael Jefferson

ALLWORTH PRESS
NEW YORK

DISCLAIMER

This book in no way guarantees employment. It is merely a guide aimed at providing information about the design industry's often-confusing hiring process.

Published by Allworth Press
An imprint of Allworth Communications, Inc.
10 East 23rd Street, New York, NY 10010

Cover design by Derek Bacchus

Cover Photo © digital vision

Interior design by Mary Belibasakis

Page composition/typography by Integra Software Services, Pvt. Ltd., Pondicherry, India

ISBN: 1-58115-421-6

Library of Congress Cataloging-in-Publication Data

Jefferson, Michael, 1982–
   Breaking into graphic design: tips from the pros on finding the right position for you / Michael Jefferson.
       p. cm.
   Includes index.
   ISBN 1-58115-421-6 (pbk.)
1. Graphic arts–Vocational guidance–United States.   2. Commercial art–Vocational guidance–United States.   I. Title.

   NC1001.J44 2005
   741.6'023'73–dc22

                                                                            2005017582

Printed in Canada

DEDICATION

This book is dedicated first and foremost to my family, who give me more support and encouragement than I deserve. It is also dedicated to the countless people who made my art school experience one that I will never be able to forget, no matter how hard I try.

CONTENTS

INTRODUCTION
My Inspiration

WHY ARE GOOD DESIGNERS UNEMPLOYED? Why is it so hard for recent graduates to find work if they have the ability to produce eye-catching graphic designs? The easy answer is that they are not applying for jobs proficiently. While the information in these pages focuses on graphic design in particular, people in all areas of design can benefit from it. Employers in every field of the arts look for the same qualities in applicants.

Before I get to the information readers really want, I will explain what inspired me to write this book. (If you don't care about that, turn to page 1 to start reading the interviews.) I decided to study the field of computer graphics after I saw *Star Wars: The Phantom Menace.* The computer effects and animation in that movie amazed me enough to make me want to learn everything I could about computer imagery. The decision to forego the Ivy Leagues, however, was unpopular with my parents, and to this day I still have not told them that my choice was influenced by *Star Wars.*

When I began the college application process, I applied to ten schools: nine liberal arts institutions and one art school. The high school I went to was a prestigious college prep school that strictly focused on academics, offering only two art classes (which explains my parent's confusion about my interest in the arts). The only art school I applied to accepted me, and I decided to attend.

My college experience can be summed up in one word: strange. Although it was weird, the school was great for me because I met people who I never would have been exposed to, and learned a lot about the field that I am passionate about. I studied everything from graphic design and 3D animation to painting and sculpture. As a testament to the program, there is a distinct difference between my work in the first year and the work I was producing at the end of my college experience. My first-year work sucked; my senior-year work was great. I wasn't one of those people who finished at the top of my class, but I graduated in four years, unlike many others. My final cumulative GPA was 3.4. I was a good student.

The summer before I started college, I began working as an intern for a contracting company, which lent the services of its employees to clients as needed. As far as I am concerned, the start of this internship marked the beginning of my design career. It was a paid internship. I worked full time for the company for four summers. Every summer I returned I was given a raise for exceptional performance the previous year. After the second summer, I began telecommuting and was able to complete projects for my job while maintaining a full course load and holding down a job on campus. I think that's pretty impressive. The projects I had to complete included everything a business would need in terms of design: letterhead, logos, page layouts, posters, Web sites, motion graphics, illustrations, promotional items, newsletters, corporate briefings, and presentations. There was probably more stuff, but that's all I can remember.

Every employed graphic designer, intern or not, probably has a list of completed projects that is just as long, if not longer than mine. I believe the thing that set me apart was simultaneously working in a group environment and through self-supervision. The group I worked for was called the Rapid Operations Communications team. We would have group meetings to understand the needs of clients and what they wanted to see in the projects we were creating for them. Once the project was understood, the team trusted me, a mere intern, to create the entire project. Once I finished a first draft, the group would meet again to critique my work. I then took their suggestions and made the changes that were appropriate. The designs were then shown to clients at meetings that I attended.

One client I worked for was a branch of the United States government, an extremely important client. If my work wasn't being done at a professional level, I would have been assigned to a different client. Every design I created was approved by the client the first time it was reviewed. I have created a lot of designs for the branch of the government I worked for, and graphics that I created can be seen all over the offices where I worked. Some of my co-workers liked my work so much that they decorated their cubicles with the imagery I designed.

My internship ended when I graduated. After I got my degree I wanted more pay and more duties. The office I worked for tried to make me understand that they didn't have a big enough budget to pay me the salary I deserved, even though three people had just gotten fired due to poor performance, not budget issues. I decided that I would rather be unemployed than continue as an intern with no potential for growth.

When I started looking for design work, I thought I would have a job in less than a month. That was foolish. At the beginning of my search I was excited about the projects I would be working on, the people I would meet, and the money I would be making. I was so excited that I had enough energy to apply for forty jobs in my first two months out of art school. I was really hoping for more than two responses. Due to scheduling conflicts I was not even able to attend those two interviews. Confident in my abilities and disappointed about the lack of interest in me, I guessed that I was going about the process in the wrong way.

After all of my education, all of my experience, working at an office where I was able to use my design skills every day, employers were telling me that they didn't want to hire me? Were they crazy? If they didn't want me, whom *did* they want? I had heard many things about what people looked for in a graphic designer, and I was tired of hearing what uninformed people had to tell me.

The majority of the jobs I applied for were listings for graphic designers. Most of them were soliciting for applicants who had three to five years of experience. The response I got most often was that I didn't have the experience necessary to fill the position. I had been working as an intern for four years doing exactly what the listings described as the duties of a graphic designer. With all the experience I had gotten during my internship, how could potential employers have the audacity to tell me that I didn't have the necessary experience? Some readers may be thinking that I didn't have a strong portfolio, or that these places were trying to make something up instead of telling me that my work was terrible. That is not the case either.

When applying for graphic design work, an artist has to submit work samples along with a résumé and cover letter. These work samples act as proof that the designer can create the type of imagery he claims he is able to create. I have often heard that the portfolio is the most important part of an application, and I always assumed that was true. Even though employers were frustrating me with this experience issue, they were also telling me that my work was good. People have told me that a high school dropout can find work if he or she has a strong portfolio. I couldn't understand why I, a college graduate with work experience and a strong portfolio, was having such a hard time finding work. If I had dropped out, maybe I would have gotten a job faster! Who knows.

With all of these myths floating around, and me not being able to find a job with the credentials I had, I decided to do something to help myself and others trying to break into the design industry. That is why I wrote this book.

The Application Process Is Painful

I have always thought that the perfect life for me would be sitting at the beach all day while my wife, Salma Hayek, fed me buckets of Popeye's chicken. I have been thinking more about my vision of a perfect life now that I don't have a job and have nothing better to do. After about a week, I would get tired of the hot sand. Salma would probably start to annoy me as all of my ex-girlfriends have after a few weeks. That's why they're exes. Eventually, as hard as it is for me to admit this, I would get sick of Popeye's chicken. What does this have to do with employment? I'll tell you. Most people think they don't want to work. That seems logical, as most people who have jobs are pretty angry and don't want to go to work. But a lot of unemployed people are also angry because they don't have a job.

Many people work simply because they need money to live. That is an undeniable fact. Aside from that, working gives people something to do. If work was only about money, why does Donald Trump still build skyscrapers? Why does Oprah continue to host her talk show? Why hasn't Bill Gates retired? Those people have all the money they could ever need, yet they keep doing the things that made them so wealthy. They need something in their lives that occupies their minds. Having a job makes people feel like they have something to offer to the world. It gives them something to talk about when people ask, "What do you do?" It is a status symbol. In many R&B songs, female singers enthusiastically sing about not wanting a sorry man that doesn't have a job. Having a job makes you a productive member of society. Employers need to respect the fact that the people who are applying for jobs are people that want to work, and, in most cases, want to do a good job.

I know quite a few people who are unsuccessfully looking for work. Myself, my mother, and the nine hundred people I recently graduated with are all in the hunt. I apply for jobs that match my experience and my mother does the same. In the opening of this intro, I mentioned my difficulty in understanding employers' criteria for experience. My mother has thirty years of experience working in her field. She was laid off from her job and searched in vain over a two-year period to find employment. That is completely illogical. Is thirty years not enough experience? The job application process is clearly flawed if people like my mother and I can't find work.

To have any hope of getting a design job, you have to know what employers look for and you have to give that to them. If you don't, your résumé will be one of the countless thousands that end up in the trash can. In addition to experienced designers who are looking for work, there are hundreds of thousands of new graduates of art programs every year, any one of whom could decide to compete for design work. That is a lot of competition.

In the midst of all that competition, finding good advice on job hunting techniques will provide applicants with a great advantage. Before I knew better, I sought that advice in all the wrong places. A few weeks after I started applying for jobs, I sent my résumé to a "professional résumé review" service. The response I got from that service illustrated to me the fact that people outside the art community just don't understand.

I was in the process of redesigning my résumé because it was outdated. The last time I had updated it was during my freshman year in college. While I was reworking the design, I wanted to get some "professional" advice on what a design résumé should look like. I received a response from the service letting me know my résumé had been reviewed two days after I had e-mailed it. The service suggested that I describe my job duties in long sentences. My research has shown that the people reviewing résumés don't have time to read long sentences. They want to read important information, nothing more. It also failed to suggest ideas I could use to make the design of my résumé more appealing to potential employers. In fact, the service suggested that I take all the design elements out of my résumé. A design résumé that fails to show one's design capabilities is like writing a note that says "Please don't employ me." People outside the art community have no idea what employers in the art and design industries are looking for. To this day I am happy I did not have to pay for that "professional" advice. Valuable information on the techniques necessary to find work as a designer can only come from people within the design community. It became clear to me that the easiest way to get to that information was by talking to people who were willing to share it.

The research I conducted was done in the form of interviews. Every person I talked to was working in the design industry at the time the interview was conducted. The interviews included in the following chapters have provided me, and hopefully will provide you, with invaluable information about the hiring process for designers. Due to limited space and time, the interviews are not transcribed in their entirety, but the documented answers to all questions are quoted directly from the various interviewees.

At the end of this book, I want every artist who reads this and desires to work in the field of design to have a better understanding of the application process. To achieve that goal, I interviewed people whose information about design employment would be helpful to newcomers. As a person who had recently gone through the process of trying to find a job, I knew which questions to ask. I asked about everything a recent college graduate would want to know regarding the hiring process for designers working in full-time positions. I also provide information about other forms of employment available to designers, such as freelance work and running a business.

I talked to working graphic designers. I found out how they had gotten their jobs and how long it had taken them to get to where they were at the time of the interview. I also talked to the people at design firms who make the hiring decisions. I learned exactly what they want to see in an application, and what personal qualities applicants have who get hired. I talked to people who started their own design businesses, who make their living doing design work. They told me about what they had to go through to get their businesses off the ground and what they wished they had done differently. I also cover the field of temporary (temp) work. I interviewed people at temp agencies to find out what they look for in people they have in their talent pool. To make sure I got a variety of opinions, I interviewed subjects from design firms of various sizes, all with varying levels of experience. To cover the experience of different regions, I interviewed people from all parts of the country. I have tried to cover every avenue of employment open to graphic designers.

The interviews were conducted as follows. A set of questions was composed to correspond to each of the three interview categories: Employed Designers, People Who Hire, and Businesses Owners. Before every interview, the participants gave their consent allowing the interview to be recorded. The interviews were then transcribed and printed in this book. Some participants chose to remain anonymous and that request was honored. The names of the companies the subjects work for are not included to avoid any legal issues that could potentially arise.

CHAPTER 1
Interviews with Employed Graphic Designers

EMPLOYED GRAPHIC DESIGNERS are just that, people who get paid to do design work. They have the kinds of jobs that unemployed designers are looking for. These people have gone through the process of looking for work and have achieved success. They have done everything that was necessary to get the job. The people interviewed in this chapter provide insight into a number of ways one can break into the field of design. One participant began as an intern, another found a job in the newspaper, and others were fortunate enough to have contacts who were willing to give them a job. These talented designers reveal the techniques they used to become design professionals.

◆ ○ ◆ ❑ ◆ ○ ◆ ❑ ◆ ○ ◆ ❑ ◆ ○ ◆ ❑ ◆ ○ ◆ ❑ ◆

NAME: Melissa Derecola
JOB TITLE: Creative Director
COMPANY DESCRIPTION: Marketing, Advertising, and Public Relations
DEGREE: Graphic Design Communications
PREVIOUS JOB TITLE(S): Graphic Designer, Marketing Coordinator
YEARS EMPLOYED IN THE DESIGN INDUSTRY: 3 1/2

Q: *How old were you when you knew you wanted to go into the arts?*
A: Growing up in a very small town, I did not think being an artist could be a job. When I was eight, I got real watercolor paper from a family friend who was an artist. At that point, art was something I wanted to do for fun, not actual work. It was not until high school that I realized art could be a job.

Q: *Was there a particular event or person that inspired you to become an artist?*
A: When I was a senior in high school, my history teacher, Ms. Fairbanks, let us do any sort of project we wanted on one of the cultures we were studying. I decided to create a newsletter about the Maya. I really enjoyed it, and before that point I had never realized that there were people who had jobs doing page layout.

Q: *How long were you without work before you found your current position?*
A: I had seven or eight months when I was employed in retail, not in the design field. I left that when I found this job.

Q: *Where did you look for job listings?*
A: The newspaper, Monster.com, and I mailed my information and samples to graphic design businesses I found in the phone book. I also went to almost all of the standard online career sites.

Q: *Where did you find the listing for your current job?*
A: The newspaper.

Q: *Did you do any research on the companies you applied to?*
A: I did some. Generally I would look at their Web sites. I wouldn't do a lot until I got ready for interviews. For the most part, I just

looked online and if they had a Web site listed, I looked up what they actually did before I sent in an application. Once I got a call for an interview, I returned to the Web site and did more research to prepare for the interview itself.

Q: *When you applied for the job you have now, what did you include with your job application?*
A: I sent a whole package in. It included my résumé, cover letter, and my sample business card, which I created. I sent samples of some of my college projects. I printed out some postcard designs and a poster, and I detailed what the projects were.

Q: *When you applied, did you add any special design elements to your résumé?*
A: I created my own stationery system for myself. I had one when I was looking for a job and I have updated it now that I have gotten further. I think that's important because if you are applying as a designer it is important to show that you can design.

Q: *Did you tailor your work samples to match the work done at your current company?*
A: I did not because I didn't really have that many samples. If I was doing it now, I would.

Q: *So you just chose what you thought was your best work?*
A: Right. Because, at that time, I only had a small selection of materials to choose from, so I just chose the best ones.

Q: *How were you notified that you would be considered for the position?*
A: I got a phone call. The owner called me and then we e-mailed several times trying to set up an interview.

Q: *How long was the time period between you applying and being called in for an interview?*

A: That was short. That was only like three or four days, because I mailed it to him, and he called when he received it. And I do know, having worked here with him, that part of it was that there were samples included. We get a lot of applications here from people requesting jobs and they just have a résumé. It's far more important to see samples and that's far more interesting. It lets us know right away whether we want to have somebody come in for a job interview.

Q: *After you scheduled an interview, how did you prepare for it?*

A: I reviewed my portfolio, because in order to graduate I had to create a portfolio anyway. So I just looked through it and made sure it was in order, checked to see if there were any projects that I would take out. I ran through my projects so that when I went in for a presentation I was familiar with them. It had been several months since I had worked on them.

Q: *What items did you bring with you to the interview?*

A: I brought a portfolio of my top projects from school. Some of them were projects that I had mailed off with my application, such as a post-card that was one in a series of five. I brought in the whole series for my presentation. I included a business card design when I applied and I brought the whole stationery system to the interview.

Q: *Did you have to make some sort of formal presentation at the interview?*

A: I did. In any interview I have ever done, I have done a formal presentation. Depending on the room and the number of people involved, I either stand up and present my pieces, or if it's a single person, I just sit there at the table with them and present my pieces. I feel that it's important to show that I know what I did and what my projects are. Having interviewed people myself, when they come and they present something and I ask them questions like, "Well why did you choose this color or this design?" and they say, "Oh I don't know, I just liked it," that tells me nothing. We need to know more because in the future you're going to have to make decisions. You can't just say, "I like the color." So I always give a presentation trying to show that I can present materials, that I have a thought process behind the materials I create, and that everything is well organized.

Q: *How much experience have you gained at your current position?*
A: I am the creative director. I do the same work, but at this point, where I am now, my position is more managerial, overlooking other people's design progress. Before, I was just doing it on my own and somebody else was looking over my work.

Q: *Do you believe that having a Web site is necessary for a graphic artist?*
A: Today, yes. Of some sort. I think that so often, when employers are looking for people, they ask for a Web site; they ask to know where they can look at things. I think that it's very important because, in a tight job market, by the time they receive samples you've mailed, they've already looked at other people's Web sites and seen samples.

Q: *Do you have any other suggestions for artists who are seeking employment?*
A: A lot of people, like my husband, when he is looking for jobs, he can go online and he can just e-mail his résumé and everything is fine. I don't feel that people in the design field can really do that. I feel that there is a better reaction when you physically mail a package, unless you are looking for a Web design job. If that is the case, the résumé, an e-mail, and a Web site seems to work. But, in any sort of print media, the e-mail résumé just doesn't seem to

give as big of an impact. Mailing seems to make sure that your piece stands out.

♦ ○ ♦ ▢ ♦ ○ ♦ ▢ ♦ ○ ♦ ▢ ♦ ○ ♦ ▢ ♦ ○ ♦ ▢ ♦

NAME: Amy Spokas
JOB TITLE: Senior Designer
COMPANY DESCRIPTION: Design Firm
DEGREE: Graphic Design
PREVIOUS JOB TITLE(S): Designer
YEARS EMPLOYED IN THE DESIGN INDUSTRY: 11

Q: *How old were you when you knew you wanted to go into the arts?*
A: While I always enjoyed art and was a yearbook staff geek in high school, I never thought I could make a real career out of it until halfway through college, when I took two design classes to fulfill an "arts" requirement. I quickly switched majors.

Q: *Was there a particular event or person that inspired you to become an artist?*
A: Professors Michael Graham and Charlotte Story at American University were wonderful mentors and I have them to thank for my career.

Q: *How long were you without work before you found your current position?*
A: This is my second position as a graphic designer. I didn't have any time off between the two jobs. But after I graduated college, I did have about six months of waiting tables and freelancing before I landed a full-time graphic design position.

Q: *Where did you look for job listings?*
A: I thought the most helpful were the AIGA (American Institute of Graphic Arts) and Art Directors Club listings. Right after college I did apply for a few jobs through the newspaper classifieds, but I felt it

wasn't effective for me. It seemed like most of the newspaper listings were for in-house positions, and I knew I really wanted studio work.

Q: *How many jobs did you apply for before this one?*
A: Before my current position, I went on between seven and ten interviews. I did interview through Aquent (a placement agency), but I didn't end up taking a job through them. I think they sent me on four or five of the interviews. I also had contacted some studios on my own and asked if they would review my portfolio. I got one or two leads from that—those studios weren't hiring, but they knew of others who were.

Q: *Where did you find the listing for your current position?*
A: I knew the principal. We had worked together at another studio, and we kept in touch after she left to start her own firm. A few years later when I was interviewing, she decided to hire another designer. She offered me the job without a formal interview, and she didn't advertise the position.

Q: *When you applied for your last job, did you believe that you exactly matched all the criteria listed in the job description?*
A: I've never formally applied for a full-time position. My first full-time job was with the studio where I had interned during my senior year of school. After I graduated, I freelanced for them for a few months, maybe one or two days a week, before they offered me the full-time position. They didn't advertise my position before hiring me.

Q: *After school, how did you decide what you would include as your work samples when applying?*
A: Right out of school, I tried to pick projects that I thought either showcased my design process or projects that I thought might have "real world" application to them. After my first job, I tried to find out

a little bit about the firm I was interviewing with–if they did mostly print or exhibit or signage–and tailored the samples I brought based on their work.

Q: *Did you add any special design elements to your résumé?*
A: What's the point of being a graphic designer if you don't design your résumé? In fact, my boss was just advertising for a position and I don't think she even considered anyone who didn't send a well-designed résumé. If their résumé looked like it had been done in Word, she didn't even call them back.

I would highly recommend that people include a few work samples in some way. Include a page of logotypes or print samples, or even the Web addresses to sites you've designed. It gives you a chance to show off your work before you've even stepped through the door.

Q: *What would you recommend that people bring with them to interviews?*
A: As professional a portfolio as you can manage. I would tell people not to be too paranoid because they only have school projects to show. I think that showing your thought process and your personality is just as important as work samples. Just make sure you're organizing your pieces in some way that looks like you put some thought and care into it.

Q: *Has the use of print production skills been required of you in your current position?*
A: Oh yes, that's a big part of my job.

Q: *Do you have any other suggestions for artists who are seeking employment?*
A: Do a little of research. Call firms that you think you would fit into, work-wise and personality-wise. Ask if someone there would have ten minutes to review your portfolio. Even if they're not hiring, they may

know of someone else who is. And maybe a month from now they will decide to hire somebody and you'll be the person that they remember.

◆ ○ ◆ □ ◆ ○ ◆ □ ◆ ○ ◆ □ ◆ ○ ◆ □ ◆ ○ ◆ □ ◆

NAME: Sean Flanagan
JOB TITLE: Graphic Designer
COMPANY DESCRIPTION: Graphic Design Firm
DEGREE: Graphic Design/Communications
PREVIOUS JOB TITLE(S): Graphic Designer, Senior Graphic Designer/ Art Director
YEARS EMPLOYED IN THE DESIGN INDUSTRY: 5

Q: *How old were you when you knew you wanted to go into the arts?*
A: I have always known that it was something I wanted to pursue. I took a printing class in high school and learned the back-end of the trade by typesetting with lead. However, it wasn't creative enough for me, so I elected to study graphic design.

Q: *Was there a particular event or person that inspired you to become an artist?*
A: My older brother Chris always told me how talented I was and to use my gift to the best of my ability. He is my inspiration.

Q: *How long were you without work before you found your current position?*
A: There was about a one-month period after graduation when I did not have work. I got a job that lasted three months after that period. When that ended, I found this job, where I have been ever since.

Q: *Where did you look for job listings?*
A: My main source at the time was the AIGA Web site. I was a student member at the time. That was the only outlet I knew of

for graphic designers. Since then I have found that there are other resources.

Q: *How many jobs did you apply for before this one?*
A: I applied to about ten after the three-month job ended and before I found the job I have now.

Q: *Where did you find the listing for your current job?*
A: On the AIGA Web site.

Q: *At the time you applied, did you believe that you exactly matched all the criteria listed in the job description?*
A: Yes, I did.

Q: *Did you do any research on the companies you applied to?*
A: If I could, yes. Sometimes they didn't list enough contact information.

Q: *Was it ever the case that you decided not to apply after doing research?*
A: Yes, there were a few cases.

Q: *When you applied for the job you have now, what did you include with your job application?*
A: Résumé, cover letter, and work samples.

Q: *Did you tailor your work samples to match the work done at your current company?*
A: Not really. As a recent graduate, there wasn't enough work to tailor to specific needs. It was a show of everything that I had done up to that point. It was a display of what I thought was my best work.

Q: *How did you make initial contact with the employer?*
A: I sent my work samples through e-mail. The résumé and cover letter were mailed. The company didn't ask for them to be mailed, but I figured the people reviewing my application would appreciate being able to hold something. You can tell a lot about people by the way they pick paper and typefaces. I think it was better to represent myself as a visual person by mailing my résumé and cover letter.

Q: *Did you include different kinds of work with the samples?*
A: Yes, I did.

Q: *When you applied, did you add any special design elements to your résumé?*
A: Not really. I tried to do a clean typeset job. I didn't want to over-embellish it. It wasn't a standard Word document, it was typeset in Quark. You could tell a designer did it.

Q: *How long was the time period between you applying and being called in for an interview?*
A: It was relatively quick, about a week.

Q: *After you scheduled an interview, how did you prepare for that?*
A: I made sure everything was in order for the interview. We had a portfolio class in school. At the time of graduation, almost everything that I wanted to put in it was already there.

Q: *Please describe the appearance of your portfolio.*
A: It was a black, standard portfolio case. All the pieces were mounted on black boards, and in sleeves. In the class I took, they had a system of how they wanted us to put the portfolio together, and that's what I followed. My portfolio had corporate identity

systems, packaging, page layout, and logo design—all of the core stuff we were being taught.

Q: *How many people did you interview with?*
A: I interviewed with two people. The first time, I interviewed with the owner. I came in for a second interview with an employee who was going to be my mentor. The interview was just to see how we meshed personality-wise, since we would be sharing projects.

Q: *Were you asked any questions that you were not prepared for?*
A: No. They were standard interview questions. At that level, there wasn't much expectation as far as job responsibility and prior history of work related to the field.

Q: *Has the use of print production skills been required of you in your current position?*
A: Definitely. I took one class in school, but it did not cover enough to really make me competent. I was more prepared than students that did not take that class. There was a lot of on-the-job training involved.

Q: *Do you believe that having a Web site is necessary for a graphic artist?*
A: I would say yes. I am saying that and I don't have one myself. I do believe that it is important, and I do need to get myself one.

Q: *Do you have any other suggestions for artists who are seeking employment?*
A: I would advise them to get a Web site. Only show what you *know* is your best work, not what you *think* is. If you can, try to tailor it to the company that you are seeking employment with. I know that's difficult for students. They might only have a few good projects, so they have to use what they have. Use all the resources available to you. There are plenty of resources available today by way

of the Internet. Try to get an internship prior to graduating. That was something that I did not do. That would have really helped me to open some doors in the design community. Stay in touch with the people you went to school with. When they go out and start working at places, it will create a professional network.

◆ ○ ◆ ▫ ◆ ○ ◆ ▫ ◆ ○ ◆ ▫ ◆ ○ ◆ ▫ ◆ ○ ◆ ▫ ◆

NAME: D. Sherene Offutt
JOB TITLE: Creative Director
COMPANY DESCRIPTION: Internet solutions and multimedia communications company
DEGREE: Fine Arts
PREVIOUS JOB TITLE(S): Creative Director, Chief Creative Officer, Vice President of Creative Delivery, Senior Designer, Design Instructor, Creative Services Director, Art Director, Designer, Sign Painter
YEARS EMPLOYED IN THE DESIGN INDUSTRY: 17

Q: *How old were you when you knew you wanted to go into the arts?*
A: I was always involved in creative activities. I don't remember making a conscious decision to pursue a career in the arts.

Q: *Was there a particular event or person that inspired you to become an artist?*
A: I guess my brother inspired me. He's always been a prolific painter.

Q: *How long were you without work before you found your current position?*
A: I have never really had a period without work.

Q: *How did you get your current position?*
A: I joined this company in '99 as their vice president of creative delivery. I worked with them for two years. At the end of those two

years, this company was acquired by another company and I decided to take a break. I left at that time and worked for an advertising agency for a while, about six months. Then I freelanced for about another six months and then I came back to this company.

Q: *Did you have to apply for the creative delivery or advertising job you mentioned?*
A: Not really. I had contacts. At the time I first worked with this company, I was an instructor at a college with two of the partners that owned the company. I had a previous relationship with one of them and he knew of my skills and asked me to join the company.

Q: *Do you believe that having a Web site is necessary for a graphic artist?*
A: I don't think that it's necessary, but I do think that it's tremendously helpful.

Q: *What advice would you give to someone when they are selecting work samples to send to a potential employer?*
A: If you are talking about someone who is coming straight out of school, most of the samples are going to be project work. I would encourage people not to be afraid to show work that is not necessarily professional work. It could be project work or work that they have done independently. I think that is fine. As far as selecting the samples, I know that a lot of work will be mockups, things that haven't actually been printed at an offset printer, but things they have made on their own. So I would say to select the cleanest presentation possible. I think it's really important when you are presenting your work that the presentation be very clean. If you've created a mockup and you've cut out with an Exacto or paper cutter, make sure edges are really clean. Good craftsmanship is critical.

Q: *Is it important for somebody applying for a design position to design his or her résumé?*

A: Yes. I can say that in the past when I have been interviewing designers, typically I would get a tremendous response. I would get a huge stack of résumés and my first cut would be any résumé that was just in Times Roman and clearly not thought out. I didn't even look at those.

Q: *What items would you recommend that people bring with them to interviews?*

A: It's important, obviously, to bring your résumé and portfolio. If you can leave something behind, that's nice. My experience as an art director has been that, typically, when I'm so incredibly busy that it's difficult for me to pay a lot of attention, I am more likely to remember people who have left interesting things like booklets or CD-ROMs behind. Even if I am not able to employ them at that point, I will always keep a leave-behind that is appealing. And then when I am looking again, I will remember them.

Q: *Do you believe it can hamper an artist's ability to be hired if his or her appearance does not match that of a typical professional?*

A: It depends. It's really a judgment call. It's important when you're going on an interview to make sure you do your homework on that organization. For instance, once when I was a freelancer, I was interviewing with placement agencies in Manhattan. I went to all my interviews in a suit. Although it did not keep me from getting offers, I definitely felt out of place because the people at the agencies were a lot more casual. I don't think it's ever really a mistake to dress professionally, but I think you have to use your judgment. I remember there was a job I wanted years ago with a company that built exhibitions for museums. I showed up professionally dressed to the interview and in that case it was a deterrent because they didn't want someone who was afraid to get dirty. Being a female and being well groomed kind of made them shy away from me. I didn't fit the role. But, that's not your typical designer situation. When in doubt, I would say dress professionally and conservatively. Not extremely conservatively. But cover your tattoos, take your earrings out, stuff like that.

Q: *Where did you find freelance work when you were looking for it?*
A: I had a long career as a designer before I became a freelancer, so my initial freelance work was with a previous employer. The freelance work I have found in my career has been through my network of being active in the design community. When I say that, I don't necessarily mean participating in director's clubs and things like that. It's just being known in the industry, working with people. When people move on to other companies, they'll remember you, they'll call you when they need design work done. So if you perform well, people will remember you and stay in touch with you for future projects. That has typically been how I have gotten all of my work, through word of mouth.

Q: *Has the use of print production skills been required of you in your current position?*
A: Yes.

Q: *How about presentation skills like cutting, pasting, and mounting?*
A: Yes.

Q: *Do you have any other suggestions for artists who are seeking employment?*
A: I would say that as far as employability goes, the thing that makes you the most employable is quantifiable computer skills. I don't say that to detract from the importance of your creativity

and ability to design, but I would encourage all people who are interested in getting into this industry to really focus on their computer skills. Do homework as to what the primary industry-standard programs are, like the Adobe Suite of packages, and stay up to speed with them. What I have recommended in the past to people who are new to the industry and having trouble being employed is that a really great way to get your feet wet is to sign up with a temp agency. There are a number of good temp agencies in the area that will give you steady work and help you with training. A lot of them provide health benefits. They test you on a regular basis, rate your skills, help you keep things up to speed, and then you get to temp in a lot of different organizations like advertising agencies and government contractors. So it gives you exposure to the potential employment landscape. You get to meet people and develop your skills and network while you are making money. You can also, risk-free, check out different work environments to see what might be best for you.

Q: *Have you gotten jobs through temp agencies?*
A: I haven't personally, but as a creative director, I have hired temps throughout the years. I know a number of people who have had successful careers working exclusively with temp agencies. When it comes to being hired for a permanent position, often the individual reviewing your résumé will be comparing you with someone who may have more experience. More than likely, the people with real work experience are going to be more desirable candidates for the job. That can be really discouraging when you're getting started. Working for a temp agency sort of levels the playing field. For instance, if I had a specific project that I needed help with, I would call an agency and say, "I need somebody who is an expert in Quark Express who can use Photoshop fairly proficiently." If you are registered with a temp

agency and know those programs really well, even if you are straight out of school and have no work experience, it doesn't really count against you; what's important are those skill sets. So you will have the opportunity to begin building your experience based solely on your skills. It helps you build that base of experience so that you can compete for the better positions.

◆ ○ ◆ ▢ ◆ ○ ◆ ▢ ◆ ○ ◆ ▢ ◆ ○ ◆ ▢ ◆ ○ ◆ ▢ ◆

NAME: Ann Jordan
JOB TITLE: Graphic Designer
COMPANY DESCRIPTION: Graphic Design Studio
DEGREE: Graphic Design
PREVIOUS JOB TITLE(S): Freelance Designer, Intern, Junior Designer
YEARS EMPLOYED IN THE DESIGN INDUSTRY: 5 including internships; 2 in full-time permanent positions

Q: *How old were you when you knew you wanted to go into the arts?*
A: I was always interested in art, but never found the time in high school to pursue it. I did a lot of work in architecture and randomly thought graphic design would be a fun field, but had no idea what it entailed. My school had both departments, so I could easily switch majors if necessary. Within the first month I knew this was the right field because of my intense passion and readiness to learn.

Q: *Was there a particular event or person that inspired you to become an artist?*
A: My parents were both math teachers, and although I could do math, I always rebelled against it. Once I was given the freedom to experience art in college, I fell in love with the idea of communicating without words in ways that are highly conceptual.

Q: *How long were you without work before you found your current position?*
A: Not very long. I graduated two years ago, and then worked for two other design studios. I recently found this company through word of mouth. I knew Christopher, a principal at the studio, who asked me to join the firm. I actually interviewed here after my graduation, but the timing was off. It definitely paid off to keep up my connections.

Q: *Where did you look for job listings?*
A: When I was searching, I looked for jobs on Craigslist.org, Commarts.com, AIGA.com, and by word of mouth.

Q: *How many jobs did you have before this one?*
A: I had two design positions as well as several internships while I was attending school.

Q: *When you were told about the position you hold now, how was it described to you?*
A: Christopher mentioned they were looking for someone to produce annual reports and other collateral, and he wanted to know if I would still be interested in working with them.

Q: *When you were applying for jobs, what did you include with your application?*
A: A cover letter, résumé, and portfolio. I often followed up with a sample portfolio for the studio to keep on file. I submitted all of these items for the job I have now.

Q: *How did you decide what you would include as your work samples when you were applying for jobs?*
A: When I apply, I hand deliver a portfolio for the people at the company to review. I would try to keep my submission between ten and

fifteen pieces. I tried to show my conceptual side as well as my professional work experience. It was a combination of schoolwork and professional work.

Q: *When you submitted your application, did you tailor your work samples to match the work done at the company you were applying to?*
A: Yes, I did.

Q: *Did you add any special design elements to your résumé?*
A: Yes. I designed my résumé, cover letter, and portfolio within the same file. I sent the same résumé with each application and tried to tailor both my cover letter and portfolio to meet the needs of that particular company.

Q: *Did you have to do an interview as part of the hiring process for your current position?*
A: Since I interviewed with them two years prior and because I had continued to stay in touch, I didn't have to interview with them the second time around.

Q: *When you interviewed with your current company the first time, what items did you bring with you to the interview?*
A: I brought my portfolio, résumé, and cover letter. I also included actual samples of schoolwork in case they wanted to look at them more closely. My regular portfolio is a mix of computer prints and photographs, all of which don't always show subtle details.

Q: *What other preparation did you do before the interview?*
A: I researched their Web site. I also looked at several of the design annuals to get an idea of what awards they had won, and what work was in the award books.

Q: *How many people did you interview with?*
A: Two people. They were both in the same room at the same time.

Q: *When you were interviewing, were you asked any questions that you weren't prepared for?*
A: No, I had interviewed for internships with several studios prior to my current position and had a good idea of what questions might come my way.

Q: *How much experience did you have in design before you got your job?*
A: I had four years of schooling. For three of the years while I was in school, I was interning. I did internships at three different places. Upon graduation, I worked for two studios as well as freelanced on my own time.

Q: *How did you find the internships you had while you were in school?*
A: I found them by looking at annuals and finding work I liked. Once I saw a studio that was doing good work, I contacted them about internship opportunities.

Q: *Was the application process for your internships the same as it was for full-time work?*
A: It was the same process, but less pressure because they were looking for a designer that had less experience. They weren't expecting me to be a great designer at that point.

Q: *Has the use of print production skills been required of you in your current position?*
A: Yes. I wasn't taught them in school, but you definitely pick them up on the job. My internships were very helpful in getting on-the-job experience.

Q: *Do you believe that having a Web site is necessary for a graphic artist?*
A: No. I don't have one. It's definitely helpful, but not necessary.

Q: *Do you have any other suggestions for artists who are seeking employment?*
A: Be persistent. Studios will not call you back; they have many more important things to do. Don't take it personally; just be sure to continue contacting them and reminding them you're out there.

♦ ○ ♦ ❑ ♦ ○ ♦ ❑ ♦ ○ ♦ ❑ ♦ ○ ♦ ❑ ♦ ○ ♦ ❑ ♦

NAME: Andrew Sherman
JOB TITLE: Senior Designer
COMPANY DESCRIPTION: Graphic Design Firm
DEGREE: Graphic Design
PREVIOUS JOB TITLE(S): Freelance Designer, Designer
YEARS EMPLOYED IN THE DESIGN INDUSTRY: 3

Q: *How old were you when you knew you wanted to go into the arts?*
A: I knew when I was seventeen.

Q: *Was there a particular event or person that inspired you to become an artist?*
A: No. I just found that it was a subject I excelled in and never became tired of.

Q: *How long were you without work before you found your current position?*
A: After school, there was about a year when I was freelancing and waiting tables.

Q: *Where did you find freelance projects?*
A: Usually through word of mouth. People I did work for in the past would refer me when they heard about projects.

Q : *Where did you look for job listings?*
A : The AIGA site. Also word of mouth from different design shops in town.

Q : *How many jobs did you apply for before this one?*
A : Somewhere around twenty.

Q : *Where did you find the listing for your current job?*
A : I found out about this company through the AIGA Web site. I got the company's address and visited them to look for employment opportunities.

Q : *At the time you applied, did you believe that you exactly matched all the criteria listed in the job description?*
A : Yes.

Q : *Did you do any research on the companies you applied to?*
A : Always. I always did research to make sure I was prepared for any questions they may have asked me.

Q : *Was it ever the case that you decided not to apply after doing research?*
A : Yes, for sure. I didn't apply if I didn't like the work, or if it looked like something I wouldn't be into. The big thing about graphic design is, not only does your personality have to match, but also your design style. The type of work has to be something you are interested in.

Q : *Did you tailor your work portfolio to match the work done at your current company?*
A : I spent a few months building my portfolio. I chose the top ten pieces, and put them in the order I wanted them to be presented in. I tried to show all the variety I could.

Q: *When you applied, did you add any special design elements to your résumé?*

A: Yes. My résumé was designed. When I was applying, I thought about the fact that ninety-nine percent of résumés are filed away for later. No one ever acts upon it right away and calls you. I decided to make it easier for employers by designing a file folder. That way, the actual résumé could hang as a folder in their cabinets.

Q: *How did you make initial contact with the employer?*

A: I have never e-mailed or faxed a résumé. I would always mail it and follow up with a call a few days later or hand deliver it. I never mailed or delivered work samples because I wanted to show my portfolio in person. I thought it was important to be able to sell my personality along with my designs.

Q: *How long was the time period between you applying and being called in for an interview?*

A: I had an interview a couple of days after I applied. I came back later for a second interview.

Q: *After you scheduled an interview, how did you prepare for that?*

A: I already had my book prepared, so I looked over my pieces. I did as much research as I could on the company. I knew exactly what I was looking for. I practiced and I looked over my stuff. A lot of it I just went with. If you are overprepared, it shows. I would wing it a lot when I interviewed.

Q: *Please describe the appearance of your portfolio.*

A: Mine was too big at the time. The actual case was big enough to hold posters. It was a giant portfolio case with individual sheets that I could take out. The work was mounted to individual art board sheets that had a clear covering around them.

Q: *How many people did you interview with?*
A: The first time it was with one. The second time it was with three.

Q: *Were you asked any questions that you were not prepared for?*
A: No, not really. I knew the type of job that I wanted when I went in there. I knew about the company. The questions that were the hardest were related to how much I wanted to be paid.

Q: *Did you do research on salary before your interview?*
A: I tried. A lot of the sites out there seem to speculate a lot. Salaries depend on the economy. They update that kind of information every year, but I still don't think they are very accurate.

Q: *Has the use of print production skills been required of you in your current position?*
A: Every day.

Q: *Do you believe that having a Web site is necessary for a graphic artist?*
A: It helps if you have a few samples of your work up there. Just enough to intrigue. If you put too much of your work up there, people have no reason to ask you to come in and show your portfolio. They never get to meet you. They just look at your Web site and put you in their file. If you have a bad Web site, it can hurt. I would only create a Web site if it's going to be really well designed. The site should be as good if not better than any other piece in your portfolio.

Q: *Do you have any other suggestions for artists who are seeking employment?*
A: Do your research. Find out what you want. Look into companies, and don't take a job you don't want. Know what you want and know what the employer wants. Don't try too hard. If you go in there and you are wearing a tight shirt, and you are uncomfortable, you will make your interview difficult. A lot of art directors, and senior

designers, and those in charge of hiring are not just looking at your portfolio, but also your personality. We get people in here who are uncomfortable when they interview. That really hurts them. If you are relaxed and act the way you will act once you get hired, you will have a better shot. You should hand deliver your résumé. Don't ever e-mail or fax a résumé. Sometimes those get discarded before your name gets read. As a graphic designer you should take pride in your work. Your résumé should be as good as any of your portfolio pieces. If you are faxing or e-mailing, it means you haven't put in the necessary effort. Either hand deliver it, or mail it in a customized envelope. Always customize letters. Find out exactly to whom you need to send it. Take the time to learn who they are. If you don't, they are not going to care who you are.

CHAPTER 2
Where to Find Work

IN THIS, THE ELECTRONIC AGE, the quickest way to find job listings is on the Internet. Here is a short list of places where listings
for design jobs can be found:

* JOB SECTION OF NEWSPAPER WEB SITES

    This is the digital version of the want ads. Most newspapers
    with mid to large distributions have job listings on their
    Web sites.

* WWW.ALLGRAPHICDESIGN.COM/JOBS.HTML

    This site is part of a portal for graphic design resources. It has
    many links to sites where freelance projects can be found.

* WWW.AQUENT.COM

    This is the official Web site of Aquent, one of the largest
    temp agencies that find employment for designers.

* WWW.RANDSTAD.COM

    Randstad is an international temp agency for people in the
    design industry.

* WWW.BOSSSTAFFING.COM

    BOSS Staffing provides employment opportunities for
    designers in the northeastern region of the United States.

* WWW.MONSTER.COM

The best-known job site on the Internet, Monster.com has a wealth of job listings in numerous categories. Design- and art-related job listings appear frequently.

* WWW.FLIPDOG.COM

A popular job site that receives a large number of new postings every day, it is highly possible that Flipdog.com will have listings for design jobs in your area.

* WWW.CAREERBUILDER.COM

The majority of listings here are not for art-related positions, but on occasion they can be found.

* WWW.DICE.COM

Dice.com specializes in listing jobs in information technology (IT). Design jobs are listed here frequently.

* WWW.WORKOPOLIS.COM

Canada's answer to Monster.com, this site has many listings for jobs in Canada.

* WWW.HOTJOBS.COM

Hotjobs.com is Yahoo!'s job database. This is another site that is likely to list a design job in your area.

* WWW.NATIONJOB.COM

Nationjob.com is a Web site for people who are seeking government jobs. There are listings for design-related positions, but they appear infrequently.

* WWW.JOBS.COM

Jobs.com has many job listings in a range of categories. The listings are broken into regions, which makes browsing easy.

* **WWW.CRAIGSLIST.COM**

Craigslist.com has classifieds for a plethora of items. Besides job listings, you can find ads for people selling everything from baby shoes to Ford Escorts.

* **WWW.COROFLOT.COM**

According to its Web site, Coroflot.com has "design jobs, designer portfolios, design sourcebook listings." It lists numerous design jobs around the world.

* **WWW.CREATIVEHOTLIST.COM**

Creativehotlist.com describes itself as having "job searches, portfolios, and recruiting for graphic and Web designers, writers, photographers, and illustrators." There are many listings here for jobs in the design industry.

* **WWW.AIGA.ORG**

The official Web site of the American Institute of Graphic Arts (AIGA). AIGA is an organization established by and for people in the design community. There are a lot of design jobs that can be found on the AIGA Web site. To view job listings, you have to become a member of AIGA.

* **WWW.ADCGLOBAL.ORG**

This is the official Web site of the Art Director's Club, which, like AIGA, is a network of design professionals. Its Web site has many art-related job listings.

When you are browsing Internet sites, remember that the people who organize the data don't understand the design industry as well as they should. These sites usually make jobs searchable by location and category. Sites that are somewhat knowledgeable place the listings for design jobs in a category labeled "Design." Other sites don't know how to categorize design jobs and so these listings sometimes end up in the "Information Technology" (IT) category. Some of the other categories include: Advertising/Marketing/Public Relations; Arts, Entertainment, and Media; and Publishing/Printing and Telecommunications. Browsing all of those categories is a painful process. The most effective thing to do is search by location and key-word. For example, if you are looking for a graphic design position, search for the phrase "graphic designer." If you are looking for Web design jobs, search for "Web designer."

Most of the listings on standard job sites and in newspapers are for in-house design jobs. That means that you would be creating work for the company, not for the company's clients. These listings are easy to find and that is why there is a significant amount of com-petition for these positions. And, because the listings are so easily accessible, people with little to no qualifications will apply. To avoid unqualified applicants, many design firms and advertising agencies choose to post on sites that draw a more experienced and talented audience. If you are trying to find a position at an established firm, browse the last four sites listed above. Not quite as many people apply to jobs posted on art-specific sites, but the level of competition is much higher.

Ways to Break into the Industry

The oldest way to get started in the industry is to become an intern. Internships at the right place and under the right people can provide you with all the experience you need to pick up a permanent, full-time job. If the people you work for like your work, they may ask you to become a staff member once your internship ends. The easiest way to find internships is to go through your school's career services office. Art schools have a working relationship with numerous places that offer internship opportunities. Another way to find internships is to browse the Web sites of places where you want to work. If they have an internship program, they will often provide information about it on their Web site.

Another way to get started in the industry is to work for a print shop. By working at a printer, you can develop a stronger knowledge of an essential part of the print design process. The printing of a design is just as important as the design itself. One interviewee said, "Once you understand exactly how printing works, you will understand how to design." You can also use printers to your advantage by developing a relationship with them.

Printers work with design firms of all sizes. The printers in your area will know who the large firms are. They will also know what happens at those firms if they have a close relationship with the people there. If you arrange informational meetings with print representatives in your area, you can discover opportunities that you may be able to take advantage of. Or, instead of arranging meetings, you can have somebody find work for you by joining a temp agency.

Temp agencies have a pool of talent they draw from when their clients need a position filled. Just like a full-time job, an application is necessary to join a temp agency. Because agencies are dedicated to finding you work, you can be a little more relaxed while you are looking for employment. When you work with a temp agency, you are also afforded the opportunity to work in a large variety of production environments. By doing that, you can discover the kind of environment that you enjoy. Temp agencies understand that somebody coming out of school does not have a lot of experience. With temp agencies, unlike applying for a full-time position, lack of experience will not hurt you, as long as your work is strong. Of course, there is a lot of competition for temp positions as well. Aquent and Randstand are two of the larger nationwide temp agencies. To find local agencies that work with designers, the Internet and the phone book are good places to start.

Starting Your Network

If you are not interested in part-time employment, another way to find a more permanent position is to start a network of contacts. By far, the easiest way to find a job is through contacts and referrals. If you know someone who knows someone who runs a design firm and that person wants to give you a job, you can get a job without ever having to look for one. After conducting the interviews for this book, I learned that the design industry is made up of a bunch of small networks of people. You will make your life easier if you inject yourself into those networks. One way to do this is to set up informational interviews, a great process for more active job seekers.

In order to get an informational interview, you would call a firm and request a meeting with the art director or another senior creative person. At these kinds of interviews, begging for a job is not the correct technique. In an informational interview, you should be asking the art director to review your portfolio. You should also ask him about what the design industry is like in his area. This type of meeting is pressure free, unlike an interview for a full-time position. There are many generous art directors out there who are willing to meet with recent graduates for an informational interview. After the interview, ask the person you met with if he knows anybody else you can talk to. More often than not, art directors will refer you to other people in the area. They might even know somebody who is looking to fill a position. If you meet with the person you have been referred to, you will then have two contacts in the design industry.

Another way to make contacts is to join the Art Director's Club and AIGA. These organizations host meetings where people who do what you want to do are in attendance and will be able to talk to you. If you make enough contacts, eventually one of them might be able to point you to a job that is perfect for you.

The easiest way to start a network after graduation is to keep in contact with the people you went to school with. These are people you already know and have a relationship with. Besides maintaining friendships, which is important, by keeping in contact, your friends can keep you updated with new job opportunities as they look for and find work. If you don't like some of the people you know, just pretend to like them so they can help you find a job!

CHAPTER 3
Job Search Strategies

FOUR YEARS AT AN ART SCHOOL can be incredibly draining, mentally and physically. (At my school, the last few weeks of the year were always like *Night of the Living "Dead."* For that reason, most students are overjoyed that they are free once school ends, and they choose to enjoy that freedom in many ways—trips across the planet, trips to see boyfriends/girlfriends, and trips to the liquor store are common choices. Students who have nowhere to go often spend their post-graduation months on their behinds. The need to do nothing is something I understand and appreciate. If you have parents who will let you sponge off of them while you refuse to find work, good for you. Enjoy that. This lack of initiative is good for people who do want to find work. If the lazy keep sitting on their couches, the active can compete for jobs in a less-crowded market.

When to Look for Work

The group of people who will be looking for work after they graduate will have an advantage in the job market for about three months. Most students choose to rest for a while after school ends and that means they will not be looking for work. While they are recovering from their educational experience, the market will have less people competing for jobs. This is a great time for industrious people to be active in the market, since some of those people who are resting may even be talented. When they get themselves together and start applying, finding a job will become that much more difficult. While it is hard to fight the temptation to be an adult with no bills and no responsibilities, applying for work in the months immediately following graduation gives you a better chance of finding work because a lot of your peers will be asleep while you are going to interviews.

Another great time to look for work is the months leading up to the holidays. At this point, many of the people who are looking for work have been looking for a long time. Around the holidays, they will allow themselves to take a break and enjoy some holiday cheer. This is a great time to jump in and steal the jobs they were looking for. The only people that have a harder time finding work than recent graduates are people who just got out of jail, so you owe it to yourself to take advantage of those months when other unemployed people are not looking.

Do You Need a Higher Education?

To be a designer, you must have some talent. That will always be true. That talent is sometimes evident in people while they are still in high school. For others, it takes longer to develop. Ability is what makes designers employable; therefore, obtaining a master's degree is not necessary in order to have a successful design career. But if after four years of college you do not have a solid grasp of design principles, graduate school may be the right path for you to take. Bear in mind, however, that if you do not have talent, you can go through six years of school and still not be employable. For the most part, employers do not give people with graduate degrees any special treatment in the hiring process. They just want to know what your portfolio looks like.

Diversifying Your Abilities

While you are in school, be it undergraduate or graduate, try to study all aspects of design that are available to you. You will set yourself apart if you are skilled in a number of mediums. Someone who is comfortable designing for the Web *and* for print will be a more attractive candidate to employers, simply because he or she is more useful. Since all designs in the professional world eventually go through a computer, it is important to hone your digital skills. You should know what the industry-standard programs are, and, more importantly, you should know how to use them. Early in your career, you will still be perfecting your skills. When you are still at the beginner level, you should know what sorts of positions you will realistically be able to fill.

You Have More to Learn

Miracle situations aside, it is unrealistic for a designer who just got out of school to expect more than an entry-level position. While you may be able to create interesting, flawless designs, the fact is that doing school projects is completely different from working in a studio environment. There are many aspects of studio work that are impossible to learn in the classroom. Some of those aspects are learning to work with clients, learning to be comfortable in a professional environment, meeting deadlines when accounts are on the line, and giving formal presentations. Until you understand everything there is to know about studio work, you will be an entry-level designer. If you exclusively apply for senior positions, you will cause yourself a great deal of disappointment.

Time to Relocate?

Location is a factor that can greatly affect your ability to find work. Finding work in small towns is hard enough without the added difficulty of looking for work in the arts. If the non-art community is having trouble finding work in your area, you will probably be without a paycheck for a long time. Relocating to a large city where a lot of design work is done will undoubtedly give you a much better chance of finding design work. It is nearly impossible to work as a designer in an area where no design work is done.

Research and Networking

The two most important things that people talked about in the interviews for this book were research and networking. By doing research, you let companies know that you know who they are, which instantly increases your chances. If you take the time to make contacts, you can get yourself into a network of people who work in the design industry, and if you do that, you will always be one of the first to know when a new position is open. Many art students don't seem to recognize the importance of networking. Don't be afraid to talk to people: you never know whom you might meet. If you get yourself into the network and do good work, your reputation and contacts will carry you through the rest of your career. Investing some time in this area early in your career will undoubtedly pay off as you continue to work in the design field. You can't sit at your computer designing all day and hope that somebody will discover you. As nice as your computer may be, it's not going to write you a paycheck.

CHAPTER 4
How to Package Yourself to Get Noticed

BEING NOTICED IS ESSENTIAL to landing a job. The qualities that employers look for in applicants undoubtedly differ from reviewer to reviewer. However, there are some universal things that they all look for. If employers look through a hundred résumés, they will give the job to the one person who stands out the most. If you can make yourself memorable, you have a greater chance of being in the five percent of applicants that get called in for interviews.

Employers in the design field require job applicants to submit a résumé and work samples. The large majority also ask for a cover letter. Many artists have never written a cover letter and don't know how to draft one. There are an equally large number of art students who give no thought to their résumés until they graduate. When going through the application process, you have to present yourself as a professional designer. You should develop a well-designed package for yourself, consisting of a résumé, a cover letter, a business card, and if you are capable, a Web site. The first client you do any work for should be *you.* Taking the time to put these items together shows that you are serious and enthusiastic about the field you are trying to enter.

Drafting Your Résumé

The first item most employers look at is the résumé. Because you are a designer and you are applying to a design job, your résumé can't look like a generic Word document. Your résumé should be a well-thought-out typographic design piece. If your résumé isn't well designed, it will likely be placed in the trash, your work samples will never be looked at, and you will never be considered. Employers have to look at a lot of applications. Eliminating poorly designed résumés is a quick and easy way to make a first cut. What employers don't like is a résumé that is too flashy, too complicated, hard to read, or too long. The following is a list of what should be on your résumé.

Somewhere near the top of the page, list your contact information. That includes your name, your address, your home phone number, any other relevant phone number (cell or work), your e-mail address, and a URL if you have one. Make sure that your contact information is easy to find. You can't get a job if they can't find you.

The body of your résumé should be separated into categories with these headings for easy readability: Education, Work Experience, and Computer (or Digital) Skills. If appropriate, add these categories: Summary, Objective, Honors and Achievements, References, and GPA.

Under Education, list the name of the school you went to, the degree you obtained, the city and state where the school is located, and the date you graduated. If you have not obtained your degree, list your estimated date of completion. You can also list any additional related training that you have gone through outside of college. It is not necessary to list any educational experiences prior to college.

Under Work Experience, list your job title, the city and state where the job was located, and the dates you were employed. If you still have the job, list the dates as whatever the starting date was to "present." Include a description of what your duties were. This can be done in list or paragraph format, and it does not have to be written in complete sentences. Listing your duties makes them easier to read. The people who review résumés browse through this information quickly because they do not have time to read long sentences. Describe what you did while you were employed as accurately as possible. These descriptions provide your potential employers with an idea of what you are capable of doing in a professional environment.

In the Computer Skills section, list the programs, scripting languages, and platforms that you are comfortable using. Do not list every program you have heard of. Be honest. Your application looks ridiculous if the list of programs you know is twice as long as your list of work experience. It is helpful, but not necessary, to break the list of digital skills into two smaller categories: Proficient in the Use Of and Working Knowledge Of. In the Proficient category, include all the programs you are comfortable using. In the Working Knowledge category, list programs that you can use with ease but have not used enough to call yourself an expert. By creating these categories, you show employers that you have a thorough understanding of your capabilities.

Under the References category, type in "Available upon request." If an employer is interested in you, he may contact you and ask for your references' contact information. It is not necessary to list references on your résumé.

The Summary is a bulleted list of your qualifications. This list should be no longer than eight items. The items on the list should be those qualifications you possess that make you a good candidate for the job. If the job requires that you be a Photoshop expert with five years' experience, include that qualification. If you provide informative descriptions in the Work Experience section, a summary is not necessary. Should you choose to include a summary, it should be placed at the top or bottom of your résumé.

Your Objective is what you hope to be able to achieve by getting the job you are applying for. While some still choose to include this, it in no way influences the employer's decision to hire you and takes up space on the page.

Honors and Achievements should only be on your résumé if you have them. Winning a pie-eating contest does not count. Include any awards or honors you have won as a result of your design work.

Listing your GPA is only a good idea if it was somewhere near a 4.0. Including a low GPA on a résumé is a terrible idea. Employers don't really care what your grades were in school if you are a person they can get along with and your work is good.

For someone who is coming out of school, there is no reason why a résumé should be longer than one page. Don't try to pad your résumé either; they get skimmed very quickly, so try to present the most important information. Print your résumé on white or off-white paper. Using neon paper that appears to glow does not make your application more attractive.

Drafting Your Cover Letter

After a résumé, the cover letter provides a little more information about you as a person and as a worker. In your cover letter, show the person reading that you are an articulate individual. It must be clear from your words that you know how to put complete thoughts together and that you have a strong understanding of the English language. If your skills in the writing department are lacking, have another person proof your letter for you.

Print the letter on the same letterhead as your résumé to give the contents of your application package a consistent feel. The cover letter, like your résumé, should be no longer than one page.

When preparing a cover letter, the importance of doing your research can't be stressed enough. Some employers understand that you are applying to a number of places and don't mind reading a letter that has obviously been sent to hundreds of people. However, after the résumé cut, many employers eliminate applicants who send generic cover letters. Why take a gamble and try to guess whether you are applying to a company that overlooks your lack of effort in this area? You should do research so that you can tell a company not only that you want to work but that you want to work for *them.*

At the top of your cover letter, list your name and address, unless it is part of your letterhead. The date should appear under your contact information and before the name of the addressee. Be sure to address it to someone. Many people choose to write "To Whom It May Concern." That instantly disconnects the reader from the contents of your letter. You appear like an informed applicant if your letter is addressed to the person who will be reviewing your application. To find out who that is, call the company and ask. If it is more than one person, address the letter to "(XYZ Company) Creative Staff." Under the name of the addressee, list his or her job title and address.

In the first paragraph of your cover letter, you should outline the skills and experience you have that make you a strong candidate for the job. Provide a few words about what you studied at college and any additional training you have received. After talking about yourself briefly, talk about the company you are applying to.

In the second paragraph of your letter, detail why you want to work for the company. When employers are looking for a new person on staff, they would rather give the job to someone who is excited to work for them, not someone who applied because he or she had nothing better to do. Take five minutes to go to a company's Web site. Browse its portfolio and find a piece you like. Mention that piece in the cover letter. If you see that the company does a lot of corporate identities, mention that you have a passion for designing corporate identity. Something really simple like that will make it much easier for a company to like you enough to give you a job.

In the last paragraph, tell the employer that you are available for an interview to further discuss how your skills and experience would fit the company's needs. Also state that if you do not hear from them by a certain date (two to three weeks later) you will contact them about arranging an interview. Your letter should close with "Sincerely," followed by your handwritten signature with your name printed underneath.

It doesn't seem like these things should matter if your work is good, but they do. You are not the only talented designer applying for a job. It is guaranteed that there is another designer out there who is applying to the same job you are and taking steps that you are not. The designer who takes those extra steps will win out every time.

Selecting and Sending Your Work Samples

If you survive the résumé and cover letter eliminations, your work samples will be reviewed. The work is the most important part of the application. After all, if you have poor design skills, you would have to be a master negotiator to convince a company to pay you to design some trash. That is why your work samples should be meticulously chosen. Many job listings ask that you send three work samples by e-mail. That gives you only three chances to convince an employer that you have the necessary talent to be an asset to the company. Here again, research must be stressed.

If a company does work for corporate clients, the employer will not be impressed by designs done in the sensibility of bondage magazines. The samples you send should not be a duplication of what the company has done, but they should have some relationship to the work of the company and its clientele. For listings on the Internet, most people will send their samples and applications by e-mail. More and more design shops are accepting electronic submissions. E-mail is cost and time effective so, in many cases, electronic submissions are actually preferred. On the other hand, since e-mail takes little effort to send, anybody can do it: if you send your work by snail mail, you will instantly stand out.

Sending work samples by snail mail gives you a physical presence. If they like your work, they have a physical print they can keep around. Graphic designers work in a print medium and it is nice if you can show that you know how to get your designs off the computer and onto a page. This can help or cripple you, depending on what you send. If you create some kind of package that is well designed and creative, you will make a great impression. If you send something that is sloppy, not thought out, handwritten, and laden with misspellings, you will kill your chances for further consideration. When a job listing asks that you send samples through e-mail, do that; however, you should also send printed samples if you have the means to do so.

The obvious disadvantage of snail mail is the painful amount of time it takes a package to arrive at its destination. By the time your sample appears on the desk of an art director, he or she has probably already gotten more than twenty electronic applications with samples included. That is why it is to your advantage to send both electronic samples and printed material.

If you choose to mail prints, make sure to let the receiver know that he or she can keep them. If you ask that your samples be returned, that places an unnecessary burden on the person who receives them, causing you to be viewed as an annoyance. Whether you communicate through e-mail or regular mail, make sure that you spell names correctly. No one likes seeing his or her name spelled wrong.

Some applicants have chosen to act as their own mailman and hand deliver their application materials. The hand-delivery technique has an advantage that e-mail and snail mail do not have. If you decide to hand deliver your application materials, you might be able to get an interview when you deliver your package. You should be prepared for a job interview if you decide to go this route.

Designing Your Web Site

By sending potential employers a link to your Web site, you are giving them another chance to learn more about your experience and your work. Designing a Web site can be difficult if you are unfamiliar with applications like Dreamweaver that are used to create them. If you are not comfortable designing a Web page, don't. Everything with your name attached to it should have a strong design. Interviewee Andrew Sherman said a designer's Web site "should be as good, if not better, than any other piece in your portfolio."

Just as important as the design of your Web site is the content. Do you want somebody who is considering you for a job to see pictures of you passed out on top of a taxicab? I would hope not. Keep your personal site personal, and make your portfolio site professional. Only put up information and work that will make you appealing to employers. That includes your name, contact information, work samples, and résumé. While you are creating your Web page, remember that the people who give jobs don't have time to waste desperately searching through your site for something useful. The most successful Web sites are those that can be easily navigated.

When you are deciding on the pieces you will put up on your site, only choose the strongest, and try to limit the number of samples on your site. If you include too many samples, employers have no reason to ask you in for an interview. Design firms separate their online portfolios into categories. If the professionals are doing that on their sites, you should do the same. Create separate categories for page layouts, logos, Web designs, etc. Arranging your work into categories makes navigating your site effortless. There should be three to five samples in each of the categories you choose to create.

Knowing what *not* to put on your portfolio Web site will help you create a site that will impress. Recent graduates and students often choose to put a biography on their site. Writing a short biography about yourself does no damage to you, but a biography is not necessary. Nobody reads them. All of the biographies I have seen on the Web sites of those new to the professional world haven't been worth reading anyway. Another unnecessary piece is the introductory movie. Unless you are trying to show off your Flash skills as a selling tool, there is no need for these movies. They take a long time to load, and they will get skipped. A splash image is a much more effective way to introduce your Web page.

Assuming that it's well designed, having a Web site is a good idea. It gives you a cheap, easy way to present your work. Instead of overloading e-mail inboxes with your entire portfolio, you can send your URL to employers. They will then, at their leisure, be able to look at more of your work.

Applying to a Temp Agency

All of the above principles should be followed when applying to work with a temp agency except for the physical mailing of samples, because most temp agencies don't like to receive printed samples. Call them before mailing anything to make sure that they will accept it.

The process involves two other steps for temp agency applicants. When dealing with a temp agency, it is important to maintain a line of communication with the people at the agency. If you don't call them after you have submitted your résumé for consideration, they will not take you seriously. They want enthusiastic people who are anxious to be a part of the design industry. After you submit your résumé, call one or two weeks later to ask if the agency received your materials and if they would be interested in working with you. After you are accepted into the talent pool, you should call every two weeks or so to let them know that you are still ready and willing to accept whatever assignment they think you would be suited for. This step is extra when dealing with temp agencies; if a design firm is interested in you, they will call you for an interview.

If the temp agency's staff decides that they want to add you to their roster, you will be asked to take a skills test. This test is designed to make sure you have the level of technical expertise that you claimed to have on your résumé. So again, be honest. If you said you know a program that you don't, your lack of knowledge will be discovered.

Will They Ever Respond?

You have taken the time to meticulously put your application materials together. You will undoubtedly have a number of questions after you submit your application. Did they get my application materials? Are they reviewing my application? What is taking them so long to respond? How long does it take to review a résumé? I could continue this list forever. When looking to fill a position, companies have a large number of submissions to weed through. They first have to get rid of all the unqualified people. They have to eliminate those submissions that don't illustrate an understanding of design fundamentals. After that, they have to make decisions concerning who will be interviewed. It is rare, but depending on the number of submissions they receive it could take up to four weeks to start the first round of interviews.

However, in my research, I have discovered that three days is the average time between submitting and being called in for an interview. If a company is interested and is able to, it will respond quickly. After a week, calling to verify the receipt of your application is a good idea. You will know that the items you sent are in the hands of the people you sent them to. After two weeks, you have every right to call the company and ask about the status of the job. If you haven't received a response after four weeks, the job has probably been filled by someone else.

Some employers are nice enough to send applicants a message verifying the receipt of application materials. Others notify applicants that they will not be considered, which allows them to look for work elsewhere. However, employers like that are rare. Busy design firms usually don't have the time or manpower required to correspond with every person who applies. It would be nice, but it's not realistic to expect every company to send you messages updating you on your standing in the selection process. If you want to know where you stand, be interested enough to call and find out.

CHAPTER 5
Interviews with People Who Hire

PEOPLE WHO HIRE HAVE ALL THE POWER. They decide who gets a job and who has to continue searching. These are the people that job seekers need to impress. Because they have the power to decide who gets the job, their opinions count more than anyone else's. They are probably the most influential people in the entire design community.

It can be frustrating to try to understand what these people are looking for. To make their thought processes a little less confusing, I asked them how and why they make the decisions they make. In the following interviews, these influential individuals reveal exactly what they look for in a new staff member. Applicants who do not take the necessary steps to stand out will never be hired by these people.

◆　○　◆　❑　◆　○　◆　❑　◆　○　◆　❑　◆　○　◆　❑　◆　○　◆　❑　◆

NAME: Anonymous
JOB TITLE: Creative Director
COMPANY DESCRIPTION: Advertising Agency
DEGREE: Advertising Design
PREVIOUS JOB TITLE(S): Designer, Art Director, Senior Art Director, Creative Director
YEARS EMPLOYED IN THE DESIGN INDUSTRY: 16

Q: *How old were you when you knew you wanted to go into the arts?*
A: I was always interested in art as a child. I decided to pursue it as a career during my senior year of high school.

Q: *Was there a particular event or person that inspired you to become an artist?*
A: My father is my artistic inspiration. He is creative and very supportive.

Q: *Where do you place notices for employment?*
A: We would first contact people who we've worked with in the past, such as freelancers or former employees. It is best to use people whom we're familiar with. They would probably be our first choice. That way we know what we're getting. Next option would be to post a job vacancy notice on Monster.com.

Q: *Where do you find freelancers?*
A: Sometimes they're former employees. Sometimes they're through staffing services. Local agencies such as Aquent, BOSS temps, and Profile.

Q: *On average, how many applications do you receive for listed positions?*
A: It really depends on the position. If it is a very specialized position, we will receive ten or more qualified résumés. If more general, we could receive a hundred qualified résumés. The economy is also a factor.

Q: *How long do you accept applications after you have posted the job?*
A: About two to five weeks.

Q: *Do you begin notifying people that they may be considered for an interview as soon as you review applications or do you wait for the two to five weeks to end before you start notifying people?*

A: When a position is ready to be filled, we'd be pursuing people immediately. As soon as good résumés come in we would contact those people by phone, have them come in, and meet them to see if they are a good fit.

Q: *If there is an applicant who doesn't have every skill listed as required in the job description, should he or she still apply?*

A: I would say yes, but it would have to be minor qualifications that they were lacking.

Q: *How much do you value the experience gained in internships?*

A: Greatly. It says a lot about the person as a hard worker willing to make a sacrifice and shows they are serious about a career. We want people who have a little bit of agency experience under their belt: experience with people, processes, the trade, media, general lingo, and what deadlines really mean. That way, less ramping up is necessary.

Q: *Is it possible for new graduates to get a job in a position that is more than intern or entry level?*

A: Entry level, yes. Intern, yes. More than entry level? Not likely.

Q: *Would you ever consider hiring a high school student if he or she had an outstanding portfolio?*

A: If there was extreme talent there I would consider it, but it'd be a long shot. I'd say that upper-year college would definitely be preferable.

Q: *Is more attention given to artists with master's degrees?*
A: For me, personally, no. I just look for talent, attitude, and intelligence. I don't care if you didn't go to school at all. You just have to have a good book and be a good match. That's all that matters.

Q: *Is experience preferred over education?*
A: Yes. Experience, talent, and attitude.

Q: *For graphic design positions, is preference given to any course of study?*
A: It really wouldn't matter what's on your diploma or what your exact major is; I would have to see what your strengths and skills are, because there's different positions within the creative department.

There are a lot of good schools and courses available. One should take advantage of getting educated by great instructors. I know I really grew in both skill and creativity a hundredfold by attending an art institute. I left there ready for the working world.

Q: *What items are necessary for a graphic design application?*
A: Résumé, cover letter, and work samples. Especially work samples. People that get in through unique and interesting ways get more attention. Maybe it's something dimensional, but the execution has to be done right. People who present things nontraditionally will stand out.

Q: *Could you give me one example of something unique that you have seen recently?*
A: I got an envelope and it was very nontraditional. There was some handwritten stuff on the envelope and some collage. I could tell the person took their time doing it. Somebody sent me a T-shirt in a box. The T-shirt had something funny on it and a cool design, and

then the stuff was in there. Just use your imagination to break through. Sending me a regular business envelope with a typed letter and a plain-Jane résumé is going to bore me.

q: *Is sending items by mail more impressive?*
a: I would probably do both. I would probably send something in the mail and by e-mail. I have a filing cabinet and if I see something that looks pretty good, I'll just stick it in my file. And that's another thing, if something comes up I'll probably go to that file first and say, "I remember that guy."

q: *Should a résumé fit on one page?*
a: I prefer short and sweet. Keep it simple, give me the facts, don't go into a lot of detail. I'd like to know your skills, programs you know, and work experience. You should prove your skill and creativity by showing me—don't tell me.

q: *Should a person applying for a graphic design job design their résumé?*
a: Absolutely.

q: *Is it the case that a poorly designed résumé can really hurt your chances?*
a: Yes. A poor design can really hurt it. That says to me poor talent, no imagination, no effort.

q: *When reviewing work samples, do you look for designs that resemble work you have done in the past, or do you look for eye-catching work of any sort?*
a: I'd say eye-catching work, breakthrough work, fresh work. I think a good creative director is going to take anybody young and out of school, knowing they're somewhat of a diamond in the rough. If a creative director can have a gut feeling about the candidate and believes that they will be responsive to advice and is

not going to get an attitude, that's something that they would look for. For instance, I went to a school's portfolio review not too long ago. There was some very good fresh stuff there. I was attracted to that because I'm forty years old now and I'm seeing that I have to make an effort to keep fresh. I have to make sure my work doesn't look like it comes from the eighties or nineties. I have to be very conscious not to do that. New, fresh stuff is very appealing to me.

Q: *When submitting work samples, is it important to display a range of work, such as logo, page layout, and poster design?*
A: Yes, but only show areas you're strong in, and a wide range is good. One thing that's beneficial to this younger generation is that you're all growing up on computers. When I graduated, the computer age was just coming in. I learned them when they started coming into ad agencies in the late eighties.

The areas that would be really good to know are both print and interactive. Know your print, know your Web and multimedia, such as Flash, and other programs. That's a leg up that the younger generation is going to have on the more experienced set. That is another area where young designers have a trait or skills over veteran designers.

Q: *Is it necessary for a graphic designer to have good print production skills?*
A: Yes. Absolutely. A lot of times if you're in an entry-level position, you're most likely going to start out doing production (prepress) work assisting more senior art directors or designers. Case in point, we have a computer artist with a good attitude and good design talent. When we're in a bind or we just want to partner up with them, they get to work hand-in-hand with the art director or designer. Sometimes it's an "I'll do one design, you do one"

kind of thing. Opportunities like that allow people to advance. If that artist didn't have good pre-production skills, she wouldn't be here.

Q: *What is the purpose of a cover letter and what are you looking for in it?*
A: I'll probably just breeze through it really quick. I would say a typical cover letter is not critical in this industry. Personally, I'd rather have something unique. It could be on a little tag or anything creative. It could even be skipped altogether if you do some interesting presentation and there's a résumé of any form. I don't care how big or how small it is—don't be standard.

Q: *About what percentage of people get called in for interviews?*
A: Less than ten.

Q: *What characteristics do you look for in someone you are interviewing?*
A: I want to see that they are listening. I won't put up with any kind of prima donna or know-it-all attitude. I'm looking for somebody who's responsive, especially if they are somebody who is younger. I've got to get a good read that they have an attitude like "I know I'm still learning and I really appreciate you giving me advice and helping me hone my skills." That kind of attitude. The dynamics of my department are very important to me. I have to consider if this person will fit in—even if they have great talent. They have to pass the personality test. I will not hire someone who is going to be a "problem child" to me or the staff.

Q: *Once interviews start, how long does it take to make a decision about the new hire?*
A: Once we see at least four or five people, we compare traits, skills, talent, and personality. Salary requirements and my budget would

also be a factor. As far as a timeframe, it just depends how urgent the need to fill the position would be.

Q: *Does it hamper an artist's ability to be hired if his or her appearance doesn't match that of a typical professional?*
A: I think it's going to depend on the culture of the place that they're going to. But to be on the safer side, I would say lean more toward appearing professional. I personally have a skepticism towards people who use "props" to look creative. I say prove it through your work.

Wearing a suit and tie is not usually expected for an interview, but I would say dress neat and show some style. You will be sized-up to pass the "presentable-to-a-client test."

If a design firm or ad agency's client base is conservative or very serious, the Gothic heroin addict look will not leave a very good impression. Our client base is pretty business minded/conservative and we have a guy here that's got hair halfway down his back and that's cool. It is OK to be a little out there. Actually, clients think it is exciting to work with creatives. I am told not to wear a tie to many meetings so I look the part. Remember, creative projects are the highlight of a client's workday. Their typical day is mostly made up of attending boring meetings and pushing papers. Interacting with someone who is unconventional makes them feel like they are in with cool people.

Q: *Do you ask questions designed to catch people off guard?*
A: No, but I do expect answers ready for common questions. I like prepared people.

Q: *How did your last or current designer get her position?*
A: A freelancer we are using who was fresh out of school. She did what I explained to you where she sent her résumé and work

samples in a unique packaging. It was something that caught my eye. I called her up and I asked her what her status was, she said she was still in school. I told her I was very interested and I said, "Hey, when you are in town, I really like your stuff and I would really like to talk to you." She did and she had the attitude that I described as very much "I'm here to learn, I can't wait to get started working." She made a very good impression. Her dad is in the business. She did quite a bit of freelance work and an internship. She had some very strong logos, layouts, and design work. She had one or two good conceptual ad campaigns, too. By that I mean the work had elements of advertisements where the visual and the headline were working together. That is something I look for. It's not hard to find folks that are good with color and type who can make things look cool or beautiful or exciting. To find folks that do something really conceptual and that has some meaning, that's a little harder to find. Conceptual pieces make a big impression.

Q: *Do you have any other suggestions for artists who are seeking employment?*
A: Know the difference between an ad agency and a design firm. Although there is overlap in what they do, the thrust of the work and culture is very different. If you are interested in either, you will probably need two different portfolios. To see the difference, get a copy of *Communication Arts Advertising Annual* and compare it to their *Design Annual.*

Do more conceptual work. Conceptual work is more challenging. Seek advice from a professional or instructor you trust to tell it to you straight. If you feel this is an area where you are not strong, just show one or two conceptual examples.

Highlight your strengths. Don't feel you have to show a wide array of media or skills. I saw a portfolio recently from a decent designer. She showed some strengths and weaknesses. There was a really poorly designed poster in there that was many years old. She put it in just for variety but it really pulled my opinion down. Don't show bad work for the sake of variety!

Seek advice from a mentor. Try to find someone currently in the field who wouldn't mind talking to you from time to time. Artists are usually really nice people and get endorphins from assisting young people. If you don't know any, see if you strike up a relationship during an interview, even if you don't get the job. Or ask if there is someone on their staff who wouldn't mind doing a little coaching. Keep it to a minimum though, you don't want to be a stalker or take up too much of their workday. Another source may be a local ad club, AIGA chapter, or designers club.

You have to break through with your work by being uncommon. You have to do something a little different than the typical stuff out there. Don't be offensive and don't be too crazy beyond what is realistically marketable. Do work that is smart and unique.

You have youth, energy, and freshness on your side: use it.

◆　○　◆　▫　◆　○　◆　▫　◆　○　◆　▫　◆　○　◆　▫　◆　○　◆　▫　◆

NAME: Mariann Seriff
JOB TITLE: Creative Director
COMPANY DESCRIPTION: Marketing and Communications Firm
DEGREE: Communication Arts and Design
PREVIOUS JOB TITLE(S): Illustrator, Designer, Assistant Art Director, Senior Designer, Senior Art Director, Creative Director
YEARS EMPLOYED IN THE DESIGN INDUSTRY: 22

Q: *How old were you when you knew you wanted to go into the arts?*
A: I never thought about being an artist as a career. I actually wanted to be an actress and started out in college with the

intention of becoming a film director. I was always doing creative projects growing up but never thought of them leading to a career.

Q: *Was there a particular event or person that inspired you to become an artist?*
A: My grandfather and my dad are both self-taught artists, so I think creativity's been passed down through the generations. But as I said, I didn't consider it as a career until I was in college and applying to transfer to film school. Two friends suggested that while I was looking at schools I should apply to an art school as well. I was intrigued by the idea but didn't have a portfolio. Luckily the college I attended allowed you to apply by completing a series of projects and submitting them. I was amazed when I got accepted. In my first week there I had an overwhelming sensation of "this is where I belong," so I guess I have to credit my friends for the inspiration.

Q: *Where do you place notices for employment?*
A: We usually post them on the AIGA Web site and the *Communication Arts* magazine Web site, primarily. There were times when we advertised in the newspaper, but we stopped doing that because it generally attracted people who had less experience. I think *How* magazine has a Web site that we have advertised on.

Q: *On average, how many applications do you receive for listed positions?*
A: It varies. I would say on average around a hundred.

Q: *How long do you accept applications after you have posted the job?*
A: It depends on how good the applications are, and how fast we find somebody.

Q: *Do you begin notifying people that they may be considered for an interview as soon as you review an application?*

A: I try to review the résumés as they come in, but that's not always possible—it depends on my workload. I have found that most employers don't respond to résumés if they are not interested in the person. When we advertise, I ask people to e-mail their résumé and samples. I ask them not to contact me by telephone. I have found that if people e-mail me it's easier for me to respond with just a "Thanks I got your résumé, no we are not interested" or "Thanks I got your résumé, we'll be in touch." I try to respond just so people know that I got it, but that's not always possible and I know a lot of employers don't bother to do that. I think it's the courteous thing to do if there is time.

Q: *If there is an applicant who doesn't have every skill listed as required in the job description, should he or she still apply?*

A: Well, it's kind of a combination of things. There are certain basic skills that you have to have. Talent is important and your personal skills are important as well. It's hard to say. The basic programs we use are Quark, Photoshop, and Illustrator. If somebody applied and they didn't have any Illustrator experience but they had a fabulous portfolio, we would certainly still talk to them. I can really tell from the résumé and a couple of samples whether I want to pursue it further. I can screen people out pretty quickly, but being a good designer means being a good communicator, and that goes beyond just technical skills, so that is really what I'm searching for.

Q: *How much do you value the experience gained in internships?*

A: I think internships can be extremely helpful and I would recommend that any student try to get one. That's how I got my first job.

Q: *Is it possible for new graduates to get a job in a position that is more than intern or entry level?*

A: There are places where you can go, for example, a small company that produces direct-mail pieces or something like that. You may be able to go there straight out of school, and if they're desperate enough they may even hire you as an art director. But that doesn't mean that you're going to get the experience and develop the portfolio you need to get a better job down the road. So yeah, you can get jobs right out of school at various levels. But really, you have to look at what you're going to learn and what kind of work you're going to be producing once you get there.

Q: *Would you ever consider hiring a recent high school graduate if they had an outstanding portfolio?*

A: Yes, I guess I would. It just depends. We had an intern here and we don't usually use interns, but this was a special case. We had an intern who was a high school graduate. She was here the summer before she went away to college. Both of her parents were graphic designers so she knew enough about the business to know what we did. She was skilled at putting together comps and things like that. She was also comfortable with the computer. We found her extremely helpful. What started as an unpaid internship ended up being a paid position, and we kept her on. She came back the following year also. It depends on the skills people have.

Q: *Is more attention given to artists with master's degrees?*

A: Experience and the quality of the portfolio matter more than the degree.

Q: *Is experience preferred over education?*

A: In most cases.

Q: *For graphic design positions, is preference given to any course of study?*
A: At first glance, I definitely take people who have graduated from a design program more seriously—especially if I recognize the school and am familiar with the quality of graduates. I have to admit to having a prejudice in regards to some of the fine artists out there who believe they can just learn a few computer programs and call themselves graphic designers. Although you need an artist's sensibilities, you have to have a communicator's heart. Good design schools train their graduates to be good thinkers and problem solvers. That said, I don't think you have to have a design degree to be a good communicator. Some of the best designers I've come across actually have come from varied backgrounds— literature, architecture, history—they've grown into design and their abilities reflect that depth of knowledge and experience.

Q: *What items are necessary for a graphic design application?*
A: Résumé and work samples. I don't necessarily ask for a cover letter, but I would expect a cover letter. If I just get a résumé without a cover letter, that would be a negative.

Q: *Should a résumé fit on one page?*
A: For entry-level positions, definitely. I've interviewed people for higher-level positions who had multiple pages and that was reasonable. But I would say for entry level, yes.

Q: *Do you prefer a short, highlight-oriented résumé or something that provides a more detailed description of past work experience?*
A: That's a good question. It depends on the work experience. It's good to show a progression of responsibility and to explain what it is you have done. If you just did production at one job, that's fine. Say that. If you did design and production at another job, that's good. It's important to be specific about what kinds of projects you worked on.

Q: *Should a person applying for a graphic design job design his or her résumé?*

A: I think that résumés should be designed to a certain degree. I have often found, especially with kids who are coming straight out of school, that most of their résumés are overly designed. I think a simple, straightforward, clean, nicely designed letterhead with a good font choice is stronger. I have had people send me some really creative little booklets or things that are almost like résumé kits. That's cool to look at, but it doesn't impress me more in terms of getting a job.

Q: *When reviewing work samples, do you look for designs that resemble work you have done in the past, or do you look for eye-catching work of any sort?*

A: I look for good, solid design skill. I look for good typography. We have an office on the West Coast. We were advertising for a designer for that office and a lot of the résumés and samples we got were from people who'd had a lot more retail experience or entertainment industry experience than most people on the East Coast had. They were fun to look at but I've never done a catalog for a skateboard manufacturer. That look is very different than the kind of work that we do. But, I can look at it and tell whether it's been well designed or not. Whether the concept is strong. I don't necessarily look for people who have had the same kind of experience as the work we do. I do have to consider whether somebody whose main experience has been with skateboard manufacturers, for example, might feel restricted doing work for museums.

Q: *Do you most prefer work samples submitted by regular mail or e-mail?*

A: I prefer e-mail by far. It's easier for me to work with and it's easier for me to file. I keep a folder of people who I'm interested in and who I might be interested in for the future. It's easy for me to contact them by sending an e-mail back. When it gets down to interviewing people,

I want to see the actual pieces. As far as first point of contact, I'd much prefer getting e-mail. Also, I know how hard it is to get samples of your work. Sometimes people send a few out and maybe they include a self-addressed stamped envelope for their return. They are important pieces and I feel a great responsibility if somebody sends me their work. I want to make sure they are returned and not damaged. But it's a pain. I'd much rather, at least in the preliminary stages, get samples via e-mail.

Q: *Is it necessary for a graphic designer to have good print production skills?*
A: Absolutely. I realize that a person coming straight out of school may not have much print knowledge. But they need to know enough to make themselves valuable to their employer from the get-go.

Q: *What is the purpose of a cover letter and what are you looking for in it?*
A: A cover letter has two purposes. One, it's proof to me that you are an articulate person who understands business, so it has to be formatted properly and make sense. What we do as designers is communicate, so it has to be well written and communicate clearly. Two, it needs to have some highlights and explain what your experience is. It also needs to show me that you know who our company is and that you've done a little bit of research on us. It should have something that personalizes it like, "I've looked at your Web site and see that you do quality work. I'm interested in working with non-profits and I see that is your company focus." That's really important because it shows that you are not just sending out hundreds of anonymous letters. You are really doing research and care about where you work.

Q: *Do you know when you are reading a generic cover letter?*
A: Yes, absolutely.

Q: *If you think you are, does that hurt the applicant's chances?*
A: Yes.

Q: *About what percentage of people get called in for interviews?*
A: I couldn't put a percentage to it. I usually do a short phone inter-view first to screen people before I take the time to meet them in person.

Q: *What characteristics do you look for in someone you are interviewing?*
A: They have to be articulate. I don't care how good a designer is; if they have poor people skills they're going to be a liability rather than an asset. Clients aren't going to want to work with them. Clients aren't going to trust them. I've had that experience with designers in the past and it's a struggle. Even if the person is a fabu-lous designer, it makes work a lot more difficult. They have to have people skills. Another important characteristic is they have to be meticulous. One thing that I see immediately is how they treat their artwork when they show me their portfolio. I watch to see if it's neatly put together, if they treat it with some sense of importance. That really does make a difference. It shows how serious people are about their work. The way they describe their work is very impor-tant, too. If they just say, "Well I did this for so and so and then I did this for so and so," it doesn't tell me anything. But if they talk to me about the thought process behind it, or what the goal was that they were trying to achieve, or some problems that might have occurred that they learned something from, that shows me that's a thoughtful person and the work is important to them.

Q: *If you interview someone and you like him and his work, do you let him know before he leaves, or is there a waiting process involved?*
A: There's a waiting process. I'll generally say, "I liked your work and I'll be in touch." In some cases, I will call them back again for

a second interview. If I like somebody else better, I may give that person a second interview first and if they take the job, I'll go back to the first person and say, "Thanks, but . . ." And so they might be disappointed because they might say, "You said you liked my work." It's one of those things where it's a process and sometimes it takes time.

Q: *Does it hamper an artist's ability to be hired if his or her appearance doesn't match that of a typical professional?*
A: Probably. I would say creativity is great, but to a point. As an artist you can get away with a bit more flair, but unfortunately, at least in Washington, D.C., conformity is the rule.

Q: *Do you ask questions designed to catch people off guard?*
A: That's a good question. Not intentionally. I might challenge someone, but I'm not into trying to trick anyone to test them.

Q: *Do you hire freelancers?*
A: Occasionally.

Q: *Where do you find freelancers?*
A: Usually they are people that I have come across over the course of the year. Maybe somebody sent me a portfolio that I kept on hand. More often than not, it's somebody who I have worked with. We've got a couple designers who've left here who are freelancing, so I call one of them because they know what the expectations are. In terms of going out, in a pinch I may go to an agency. But I try to avoid that.

Q: *Any reason why you avoid agencies?*
A: If we had an ongoing relationship with an agency, I would probably feel like they understood what we really needed and sent us the

right people. But in many instances in the past, we've had people come in from agencies and they either weren't as qualified as they were made out to be, or they didn't understand the project, or it just didn't quite work as well. I would rather develop my own personal relationship with somebody and know their work and call them up when I have a job that's appropriate for them.

Q: *Do you welcome submissions from people looking to do freelance work?*
A: I don't go out looking for it, but yes, if somebody sends me something that strikes my fancy, I'll keep it on file in case I have the need.

Q: *Where do referrals rank on the totem pole of potential employees?*
A: I would definitely take a job candidate who was referred by someone I know more seriously.

Q: *How did your last or current designer get her position?*
A: We advertised and she contacted me. We went through the interview process. I interviewed a number of people from out of town also. It was an entry-level position and I was looking for a pretty specific set of skills.

Q: *Do you have any other suggestions for artists who are seeking employment?*
A: If you don't have a lot of experience, do whatever it takes to get some experience and some work in your portfolio. Register with an agency if you can't find a full-time job. It's a good way to learn if you can get out there and get into different studios. But it is far better to do entry-level work at a company that is doing great work—so you can be around it and learn—than it is to work at a higher-level job where no one around you is better than you. Use your first few years to soak up as much experience and as varied

experience as you can. And when you do apply for a job, realize it takes time. Sometimes it can take a month or two to go through the whole process. Between collecting the résumés, contacting people, setting up interviews, that kind of thing. You have to be patient.

◆ ○ ◆ ▫ ◆ ○ ◆ ▫ ◆ ○ ◆ ▫ ◆ ○ ◆ ▫ ◆ ○ ◆ ▫ ◆

NAME: Mike Raso
JOB TITLE: Senior Designer/Art Director
COMPANY DESCRIPTION: Full-Service Design Studio
DEGREE: Visual Communications/Graphic Design
PREVIOUS JOB TITLE(S): Graphic Designer, Senior Designer, Art Director
YEARS EMPLOYED IN THE DESIGN INDUSTRY: 19

Q: *How old were you when you knew you wanted to go into the arts?*
A: When I was a sophomore in high school.

Q: *Was there a particular event or person that inspired you to become an artist?*
A: My high school art teacher was a big influence on my decision to become a graphic designer. He was very supportive and explained the possibilities of a career in the field.

Q: *Where do you place notices for employment?*
A: We would do a posting through the local chapter of AIGA. That's definitely one thing we would do first. Then it's also word of mouth and going to schools as opposed to just doing a general listing. We have done general listings in the newspaper. The problem is people don't tend to read your description of what you're going for. If you're asking for somebody with three to five years of experience,

we've had people respond with twenty-five years' experience. So there was a really large disconnect in terms of the résumés we were getting back. So now we tend to be more focused. We would go to a school or talk to a professor or list it at AIGA or do word of mouth. We found out that people just didn't read the fine print. The newspaper ads were so encompassing that you got second-year people that were still in school responding to a job asking for three to five years' experience. You have to wade through a hundred and fifty résumés and then ninety percent of them aren't even applicable to what we are shooting for. We have sort of taken a different route in terms of hiring our creative staff. We have done some portfolio reviews at some of the local schools. We haven't hired lately. The last hire we had was somebody we had on as full-time freelancer. She was here four or five days a week for six hours a day, but as a freelancer. Obviously, you know how the market was three years ago, and then the bubble burst. Luckily, we weren't hit that hard.

Q: *On average, how many applications do you receive for listed positions?*
A: When we were doing the listings, we would literally be inundated. Before it got to me, I would have the office manager look through. If we were asking for three to five years' experience, at least to go through the first hundred that came in. It was more office manager–type people responding to the design jobs. It was really very odd and that's why I basically didn't have the time. So our office manager would sift through the first hundred and then maybe out of there pull five that met the description in terms of skills and amount of experience, has worked with these programs, and has worked in a studio.

The times when we were looking for folks more actively was when the market was really bad. The economy had just taken a downturn and a lot of people were out of work and were willing to apply to a lot of things that maybe they weren't suited for, or had the skills for. I was totally floored by the number of résumés that responded. We had to have some system of filter. You would sit there and open up a hundred résumés while I still have to be billing and getting my jobs done while working with my clients. I was doing it all after hours when the phones weren't ringing. Out of the applicant pool, our office manager would pull maybe five. At the end of the day I could take an hour and go through and maybe check out their sites, or look at their samples, or whatever they had sent. That was a little more efficient use of time. Then we brought some folks in.

We do hire freelance designers when we get totally overbooked. Like this project that's coming in, it's going to be really tight for the three of us to do all the work because there are so many deliverables. We have a good stable of folks, illustrators, and designers that we work with on a per project basis. That's actually how we've been handling a lot of jobs that come in at the same time. We take a very reserved stance about bringing another designer on staff. Just because we have to see the outlook for a year, that the work will be there. It's not fair to bring somebody on and three months later say, "Thanks for coming onboard, but we misjudged and we don't have the work for you." We've all been on the other end of that. Our most recent designer worked with us for a year before she technically became a full-time employee. It's a much more calculated and slow approach, but it's worked out great. When we do get slammed, we have relationships with other designers that we can pull right in who know our approach and what we do. We're not your typical studio in that regard. It's a more thought-out, methodical process, about bringing somebody onboard.

Q: *Are the freelancers you bring on mostly people you already have a relationship with?*
A: Yes. Or it could be more targeted. For a while, we had three really large Flash projects in. That's a very targeted expertise. We

happened to come across, through word of mouth, somebody that was too booked to help us. He said, "Check out this friend of mine." He actually ended up coming here for a month. It was so much day-to-day interaction. Some of our contacts aren't even in the area. We do it through posting up comps and e-mailing PDFs. It could be in the sketch phase, like you see around the office. We do tons of corporate identity. To just shake it loose a little bit, we give somebody a design brief and say spend five hours on it. They come up with a completely different approach and we'll have maybe a few more pages of sketches. So we are very open in terms of getting the ball rolling.

Q: *If there is an applicant that doesn't have every skill listed as required in the job description, should he or she still apply?*

A: Absolutely. The skills listed in the job description are what the applicant would have in a perfect world. I don't know everything I should know. Nobody does. It's more of the basic skill set and, unfortunately, it all comes back to, obviously, the programs now. We actually look beyond that. We look at portfolios, it is more about your process and how you dissect the problem and come up with the solution. I am not an illustrator, but if I want to illustrate something to solve a problem, I'll hire an illustrator. If I am not a super Photoshop guy, I do the basics, but if I am doing a photo collage, I'll hire somebody to do it. It's more efficient and actually you get a better product if it's somebody's forte. We are constantly doing that. If we want this style of illustration for this logo, we've got people that are really good with a particular style of line illustration. We'll fake it for a comp, but if it's a go, we will actually engage somebody to do it. That way, it's on them. I'll manage it, and in the meantime, I'm on to the next thing.

I guess the overriding factor would be an amount of years we were looking for in somebody. There's a different skill set in somebody that's right out of school versus somebody who has worked for five years. There's certain assumptions in terms of dealing with clients and how you gauge your time with multiple projects. You can spend as much time as you want on a school project. When you're working here, some of the projects have different budgets. You might only have five hours of creative. You cannot spend twenty hours on that project because we're in a loss now. That is the biggest switch for a lot of people I have met and talked to. We don't want a person to lose their enthusiasm for exploring, but you still have to work within the project. There are a lot of projects that we only have fifteen hours to complete. We go over. Everybody goes over, but you can't spend forty-five hours on a fifteen-hour project.

This new rollout we're having is a very large budget, so the time factor is when we get it done versus the amount of time we can spend on it. Somebody who's out of school, or who's been out for one or two years is still probably learning their way in terms of a studio situation. You have certain expectations with different levels of experience. That's kind of like with any job. Somebody that's been working for ten years, you're going to expect to come in and we'll say, "We want you to make this presentation." That's not a big deal. But if you tell that to somebody that's right out of school, that's going to be pretty daunting. If you say, "I want you to present in front of five clients," they'll say OK. . . . They don't have the experience with clients. That's fine because if we were looking for somebody with less experience, we would be looking to see how quickly they could develop. Usually what happens is once they're around other folks and see how they work with clients and work with presentations, they tend to pick it up and add their own elements to it. To answer your question, you don't find somebody that's a Flash expert and a Photoshop expert who can present and has super conceptual skills. They would probably have their own company. It's kind of a dream list, and you work from there.

Q: *Is it possible for new graduates to get a job in a position that is more than intern or entry level?*

A: A lot depends on the book. I have seen an increase in the quality of portfolios right out of school, in a very large way. Senior position, that's a little bit of an ambiguous title. That could be three years, or five years. It doesn't have to be twenty. If somebody is looking for creative director, that becomes more messaging and marketing. You have to be able to discern, not just, "I like this design." It's more about what the marketing message is behind it. A creative director has a little more understanding of how the creative of print, Web, and TV fits into the complete corporate picture. That does start to get on to more marketing issues. Maybe you are very talented in corporate identity and branding and that's something you really excel at. But being right out of school, you would have to have a really exemplary portfolio. I have seen some incredible work that's come out of folks that have just graduated. There was kind of a downturn when everything began coming from computers because a lot of courses were focusing on programs instead of design theory. Thinking was removed from the work. Maybe seven years ago, there were these incredibly technical portfolios, like, "Look what I did." I'm like, "What was the message, what were you trying to say, what were you trying to solve?" I would say in the last few years it's really kind of swung the other way. I have a friend that teaches undergrad design. We always get into these discussions about how he teaches his class. A lot of the folks and his cohorts, they don't let undergrads touch a computer. The first couple of classes are visual communication. Theory about problem solving, about looking into an issue and which direction you want to go. Not "OK, I want to do this on a computer." It has been interesting to see how folks in the education field have tailored their curriculum. I am definitely seeing a change in portfolios of folks right out of school. I think it's gotten a lot stronger.

Q: *Is more attention given to artists with master's degrees?*
A: Actually, I would say no. My impression is if you are getting your master's, you are probably going to want to go into teaching. Personally, I have an associate degree. I have a two-year degree in visual communication. But I have eighteen years of working in studios. We've had folks who've worked here going for their master's. Three of them have gone back to teaching. It seems with my experience that it's more of a springboard into the educational aspect of it. Folks would tend to get their undergrad work for three or four years, get practical knowledge, and then go back to school. That way, at least if you are teaching you didn't go directly from undergrad to graduate to teaching. Because then, as a professor, had you actually worked in the field? And had to work with budgets and personalities and different clients? So the answer personally would be no. It's something that's impressive, but it's more about what's in your portfolio and your people skills. We deal so closely with our clients. The old people think the designer goes away in their little cube, puts their headphones on, and doesn't have any interaction with the client. Markets are so competitive now. If you have a master's, that's great, you can bring more to the table. But if you have an associate's degree and you can still get your mind wrapped around a project, you can still be available.

Q: *What items are necessary for a graphic design application?*
A: Résumé, cover letter, and work samples. A good-looking, readable résumé. Then I look for maybe some handouts, look at some

samples, maybe somebody has a Web site I can go to. All of our clients are on our Web site. That's another thing that I don't think enough students do when they get out of school. It doesn't take much to go look at a company and see that they do this or that. You should tailor your letter or your approach to that. There are folks that do more entertainment work. If you are working for Viacom or you've done some MTV work or something that's a different attitude than us. We do work for Fannie Mae. Now with the computers, it doesn't take much to spend a few minutes and to tailor that cover letter. "Oh, I saw the work that you did for Fannie Mae and I feel that my skills would be applicable in your office environment because of the work that you've done." Instead of just a form letter, put in the name. It doesn't take a lot, and I think that's the difference when certain folks rise to the surface. It's nice when I can read the résumé, it's well designed, but it's not on neon paper, and I don't have to turn it sideways. We want that on certain projects, but everybody's busy. If a firm does law firms, you would probably take a different slant on your cover letter. I'm not saying redesign your résumé every time, but if it's somebody whose got a little more music industry, maybe you can push the résumé a little bit further. Still you have to be able to read it.

Samples are great. Even just 8 1/2 × 11 handouts if it's identity or brochure work. Or attach some PDFs with an e-mail résumé. Web sites are great. If you are pitching that you are a Web designer, you should have a very workable portfolio online. But if you are more coming from the print aspect, make small handouts. Not the whole portfolio—three of your best. A lot of people call in and say, "Can you look at my portfolio." I always make time for people. Usually the problem is they will put seventy-five things in the portfolio because maybe they are only out of school for a year or two. I would often say "Your work is good, but have a quarter of this." A lot of the folks coming up say, "I can't show this because it wasn't printed at a studio." Well, still, if it's a school project or personal project, put in three, four, or five of your strongest pieces. Because that's all that we are going to remember. By the time I get to the fiftieth piece, it's kind of hard to remember the pieces that stood out. That's one point of doing a little bit more homework. It gets more competitive every year. That's what I try to tell people. If you walk in, it makes the biggest impression if you know that the company does a certain amount of work for a certain audience. Maybe you could put a few more samples of that in your portfolio, and put that up front. It shows a little more initiative. I would never expect an applicant to ask me about this company, because it's all on our site. What we do, who we work with, who's here. It's all public knowledge. I get a little put off by that because, man, you didn't even surf around for ten minutes!

Q: *Do you prefer work samples submitted by regular mail or e-mail?*
A: It doesn't really make a difference. The thing about getting the actual piece in is that from a print standpoint you can see what kind of paper they designed it on and how they did their presentation on their handouts. If they put in an interesting presentation piece—I'm not talking bells and whistles, but how you actually send the letter and the samples—that's a pretty important thing. It's the little things, like if you didn't even back it up and you stick it in an envelope and I get it and it's all damaged. Also, how's the label addressed? You don't just hand write it. It's those small things. It doesn't have to be super kitschy or overly designed. You almost can get a sense of somebody, as opposed to e-mail, by the way the whole system looks, and how they are presenting themselves. How I get that package is an indication of what kind of designer you are. Basically, this is a system of you. You are sending it to me, another design

professional, and you must take time to do X, Y, and Z. That's why I like to get actual samples.

Q: *About what percentage of people get called in for interviews?*
A: Well, going back to when we were looking a little bit more, we would probably pull in maybe five to seven percent. That's when all the things would come into play. How do samples look, what the history is, does this person fit what we're looking for a little more in terms of the résumé and what's on their résumé. It's a pretty small portion because it goes through myself, the other art director, the president. We bounce it off quite a few people at that stage. There's usually a phone conversation or something. We would never really bring in ten people because we would just try and make a little more efficient use of everybody's time. Maybe two people are really close, and we'll bring them in. Or these three or four people are close and you do a forty-five-minute interview or something like that. I would meet generally first. We would then bring in the other art director, the other senior designer, or the president, to meet after myself. That way we can sort of gauge whether I was mistaken or missing something. There's always a second interview.

Q: *What characteristics do you look for in someone you are interviewing?*
A: I would say the first characteristic would be that no matter how far out of school, they are not afraid to express their ideas. There's no need to be timid. In a meeting we just had, three fourths of the ideas we laughed at because they were so bad. But one of them led to where we wanted to be after a two-hour meeting. It was based on a terrible idea. We knew it was terrible, but we were just throwing things out there. That would be the first thing. Obviously, you are going to have the talent to work here. You are going to have the strong portfolio. You have some

problem-solving skills. A lot of our work begins with sketches. We want someone who is willing to share their ideas openly. We tend to work with four people together throwing out ideas, seeing what works. We do go away on our own and bring ideas together, but what I would look for would be somebody who can really just step right in and not be afraid to contribute. No matter how good or how bad. You'd be surprised—a lot of folks don't want to do that. I didn't want to do it on my first few jobs. You might sit there a little bit more quietly, a little bit more passive. You might have been thinking, "I kind of had that idea." You shouldn't be afraid to throw it out there. We are all about getting the work done, getting the work done efficiently, being profitable, and creatively trying to keep everybody happy.

Q: *Is it important for designers to have good print production skills?*
A: Absolutely. Ninety percent of the time, we buy the printing for our clients, which means we are the ones who prepare the files and pick a printer, go out on press checks, manage it all. Ten percent have their own production people. Even with that, we try to tell them which printer to go to. Ultimately, if this piece doesn't come back nicely, we can't put it in our portfolio. The print production has to be spotless. If we are not buying it and it goes to a printer and there's a problem, it's going to come back to us. Like I said, we buy ninety percent of our printing and we deal with twenty different printers. We actually get complimented on how we set up our files that go to the printer. That's something that shouldn't even be an issue. It should be super clean. The printer should be able to take your markups, your CD, and go right to preflight. Maybe they'll have a couple of questions—like "we can do a four-color black instead of this solid black to make it richer"—and other production ideas that they can bring to the table. There shouldn't be anything about missing fonts. Or this is set up, you are reversing sans serif

type at six points out of a four-color build, you know it's going to plug up. You should know that by now. In terms of preparing files, you have to make sure you don't get calls from the printer unless they are about making something better. You have to have those skills as a given.

Q : *Do you have any other suggestions for artists who are seeking employment?*
A : First thing, definitely do the background. Be out there at AIGA events. You just talk to people. You can't be afraid to be out there. My last two jobs weren't through the paper. They were through printers that I knew that said, "We're looking for somebody with about your experience because one of our clients needs somebody." If I start to look for another job, I am not going to look in the paper. Those are going to be more in-house positions. If they're going to list it, they are going to get hundreds of responses. It's a good way to go in terms of getting your foot in the door and getting your first job. I would suggest affiliation with the local AIGA chapter. Contact the printers in the area who aren't quick printers, printers who are the four- to six-color printers, if you are going to get into some corporate work. Call and ask to speak to an account executive at the printer. Show them the portfolio, because if they like it, it's a big cycle. If that prospective client goes, "Man, I need somebody that's got two or three years' experience, but I don't want to run an ad because I don't want to get six hundred résumés," I am going to ask my printers. That printer might say, "Oh, I have a person you might want to talk to." If you end up being hired, I can guarantee that that printer is going to get another job because they helped their client.

Also, call agencies whose work you like and ask for informational interviews. Don't call and say I am looking to be hired. It's funny, everybody's busy, but unless I'm really slammed, I have no problem taking forty-five minutes out of my day to talk to somebody who's trying to get started. Most designers and art directors have been in that position, and understand that, and will do that. Ask for informational interviews. But go in doing your homework on their site. "I saw the annual report you did for XYZ Company. I'm out of school, I'm new to the area. Would you have half an hour to meet with me? I'd like to get your thoughts on my portfolio and the design market in your area." You're not saying, "I need a job." Always ask, is there anybody else I can talk to that you know? I know other art directors and designers in the area. I have been here long enough. Just get a couple of names. For instance, I'll say, "Give my friend Howard a call at this studio." He might not be hiring, but you can go talk to Howard. Shake enough trees and something is going to fall out. Somebody is going to say "There is an opening here."

There are a lot of classes graduating every semester, with a lot of talented designers. But the great thing is it has really opened up with the Web. It has actually opened up a lot of venues for a lot more people. The main thing is getting your foot in the door, working for a year or two and building your portfolio. Start replacing those school projects with print projects. Most art directors are going to understand. When you show your first book, we don't expect you to come in with ads that were running in *Time* magazine. It's kind of understood that you are going to work your way up.

◆ ○ ◆ ▢ ◆ ○ ◆ ▢ ◆ ○ ◆ ▢ ◆ ○ ◆ ▢ ◆ ○ ◆ ▢ ◆

NAME: Victoria Coulter
JOB TITLE: Company does not assign job titles
COMPANY DESCRIPTION: Design Firm
DEGREE: Illustration, Fine Arts
PREVIOUS JOB TITLE(S): Freelancer, Principal, Partner
YEARS EMPLOYED IN THE DESIGN INDUSTRY: 19

Q: *How old were you when you knew you wanted to go into the arts?*
A: Sometime in early childhood.

Q: *Was there a particular event or person that inspired you to become an artist?*
A: Since I don't recall any specific life-changing event, I'll just have to give life itself the credit!

Q: *Where do you place notices for employment?*
A: We have not needed to. We have a well-established portfolio review policy. We review portfolios every Wednesday, regardless of whether we are hiring or not, and invite photographers, illustrators, and designers to come by. We have a good number of résumés on file of people who are looking for work. If they haven't found it, that's where we start when we need someone, because we've already seen their portfolio, we've met them, we know if we like them, and if we'd love to work with them. If we had to advertise, we would probably post at the art schools. We've never listed a job in any of the big journals.

Q: *Should a résumé fit on one page?*
A: It's ideal. If it's a very well-organized résumé and it needs to go to two pages, because somebody has had a lot of work experience, I don't see why it shouldn't. But for somebody who's coming out of school, somebody who has worked for less than five years, any more than one page would be excessive.

Q: *Do you prefer a short, highlight-oriented résumé or something that provides a more detailed description of past work experience?*
A: I am a big fan of listing both the job title and a brief description of what the applicant was responsible for. I want to know what the

job's responsibilities were, rather than simply saying "junior art director," "senior art director," etc. Different titles mean different things at different firms. Providing a description also gives us an idea of how articulate the candidate is in terms of discussing the job, as well as what it really was that they did.

Q: *Should a person applying for a graphic design job design his or her résumé?*
A: Yes.

Q: *When reviewing work samples, do you look for designs that resemble work you have done in the past, or do you look for eye-catching work of any sort?*
A: I look for great work. It absolutely does not have to match the kind of work we have done. We do have a lot of corporate clients, so if somebody had a really heavy-duty CV and résumé but was not particularly interested in developing a more corporate style, I might question whether they would be comfortable. But I wouldn't throw their work out. If it's great work, it's great work.

Q: *Do you most prefer work samples submitted by regular mail or e-mail?*
A: I prefer to see work samples in person. I'd rather be able to ask somebody about their samples and discuss the work with them. We don't have a drop-off policy. We want to meet people. I may be intrigued with somebody enough to bring them in by seeing samples of their work. But ideally, I would rather meet the person, because the work is part of the story and who the person is is really important.

Q: *So you welcome people that want to schedule interviews?*
A: We have a portfolio review every week. That's just part of what we've done. I don't think every studio has that.

Q: *Is it necessary for a graphic designer to have good presentation skills?*

A: Yes. We've had people work for us in the past who have been terrific designers, and knowing how to present themselves—how to structure a résumé, how to put together an effective portfolio—was not something that they learned in school. I don't know why, and honestly I find it surprising. I think that being able to present yourself—being able to design your résumé or your business card—is an essential way to show who you are as a designer and to show what your personal aesthetics are. There is a certain amount of craft required, which is one of the things that I think has been underplayed in teaching—solid, hands-on ability to design. It isn't all about computers. Computers are fabulous and they are wonderful tools. We couldn't do without them. Even so, there is a certain amount of craft that goes with good design. I don't consider it essential, but I sure consider it handy.

Q: *Is it possible for new graduates to get a job in a position that is more than intern or entry level?*

A: Something like a senior designer, probably not. I don't think anybody should really expect that. I wouldn't. There's a lot of skill, and working with people, and directing a team, and being able to work with clients, that you have to learn by doing.

Q: *Is more attention given to artists with master's degrees?*

A: No.

Q: *Is experience preferred over education?*

A: Absolutely. We all know that you learn about a hundred times more in your first year of working than you do in school. I love school, we're glad it's there. But here you really learn what you're doing.

Q: *What is the purpose of a cover letter and what are you looking for in it?*
A: A cover letter, if you are submitting your résumé by mail (which does happen sometimes), is a way of introducing yourself beyond the résumé. It's an opportunity to say you're not just doing a scattershot approach: "Hi! I am sending this to everybody in the work book and I'm sending this to everybody that has a Web site." A good cover letter transmits the message: "I bothered to look at your Web site," or "I am familiar with your firm," or "I've seen such and such a project." A good letter gives you the opportunity to say whatever it is you want to say that explains why you want to work for that firm. For example: "I've gone through your Web site and I'm totally impressed. I noticed that you do a lot of identity work and that's one of the things I am most interested in. My résumé is attached, I'd be happy to set up an appointment." Again, it's an opportunity to present yourself as an articulate, professional person. Any opportunity you can take to do that is going to help. It's silly because it seems they are all things that have nothing to do with design, but they do. They just do.

Q: *What characteristics do you look for in someone you are interviewing?*
A: How somebody works with type. How well they understand type. How it's part of the coloring of the page. That's one of the most important things. It's something that somebody has to have a good feel for. I think it can be developed in school, but I don't know if it can be taught. It probably could, but the teacher would really have to know what they were doing. Type is really important, and the ability to balance a page. How well does the layout direct the eye around the page? How well does it communicate? How well does it identify what the subject is about? What is the nature of the work being presented? Is it appropriate? Is it exciting? Even if it's a really rough piece—say it's really down and dirty,

like a truck design or something—is it well presented? If somebody managed to set something apart that doesn't look like every other piece we've seen designed for that same industry, that's what we look for.

Q: *How about personal characteristics?*

A: It is really nice if somebody is articulate. I think it's just as important with designers as it is with somebody who's going to be a lawyer. They have to be able to speak well for themselves and be able to explain what it is they do without too many "ums" and "ers," barring normal nervousness. An understanding of why they chose to be a designer. One of the most important things we do as designers is communicate. Communication is not simply the ability to do killer Photoshop. It's very much the ability to understand in verbal concepts what our client needs and be able to explain that back to them—with any luck, better than they did themselves. Sometimes clients don't understand what they've explained to you. It's important to be able to present it to them. Ask intelligent questions. Do you know what you are talking about? How can you possibly design for somebody in the real world if you don't understand what it is that they need? So we do look for verbal communication skills. Somebody doesn't have to be Einstein, but they should know what they are doing, and why. And they should be interested in more things than design. "Well rounded" would be the best way to put that.

Q: *Does it hamper an artist's ability to be hired if his or her appearance doesn't match that of a typical professional?*

A: No, as long as they are willing, if they are going to client meetings, to dress for the occasion. I don't care if they come in with jeans and three pierced body parts. It's fine with me. If they are a good designer and they are courteous, pleasant, neat people, I want to work with them. However, if they're not willing to dress in a more corporate fashion when needed, they probably won't be accompanying us to meetings!

Q: *If you see someone and you like him and his work, do you let him know right away or is there a waiting process involved?*
A: It has worked both ways. Sometimes we've had to think about it because we've had more than one candidate who's been terrific, and then we really have to make that hard decision. Who do we think is going to be the best match for our shop at that point? It wouldn't always be on the spot. A while back, we were reviewing somebody's work when we were doing a lot more annual reports. She had one of the best annual report portfolios I had ever seen, then or since. It was spectacular. "When can you start? Right now. I don't care if anybody else has offered you a job, you are starting now." That was just great. When it hits, it hits. For the most part, we like to talk about it. I'll speak to the person, my partner will speak to them, and other staff members will speak with them. We are a very tight team.

Q: *How did your last or current designer get his or her position?*
A: Through the review process.

Q: *Do you have any other suggestions for artists who are seeking employment?*
A: I would say that how you put your portfolio together is critical. Your portfolio should be put together as professionally as you can. Not everybody has our policy, not everybody is going to meet somebody in person. Some people are going to drop it off; some people are probably going to send it by mail. So it's got to be beautiful. I've seen pieces that were hand assembled because someone was just coming out of school. They couldn't afford to spend four

hundred dollars to buy a fabulous, ultra-cool portfolio at some art store. They put together something on their own, and some of them are outstanding. If it's creative, if it's beautifully done, that shows imagination. That's going to get attention. Again, that's showing what somebody can do when they're working with a budget, which is important. Not all clients have fabulous, rich budgets. There are people that come to you with five hundred dollars and say, "I need a brochure." What are you going to do, throw them out? You work with them the best you can. You tell them what you can realistically do and you work with them. I think somebody presenting themselves in a way where they show themselves to be creative, thoughtful, professional people goes a long way toward establishing themselves as professionals, even if they're just out of school.

Do everything you can do to get an edge. That's how you put your portfolio together. If you've only got three great pieces, just show three great pieces. Never pad it with a million things just to show that you've done a ton of stuff. If seventy percent of it is OK, don't show it. Show a great thirty percent. I'd rather see that, and I think other designers feel the same way.

I love to see a résumé that somebody really put some thought into. And for heaven's sake, spell check! Seriously and truly, it is one of the saddest things that I see, and I see it way more often than I wish I did. Make sure that the *P* in Photoshop is capitalized. This is dopey stuff, but it reflects poorly on a candidate. There are some really talented designers coming up these days. You've got to be able to set yourself apart. When someone interviews you, send a thank-you letter. Make sure you spell their name properly.

I'll never forget one time, when we were sharing design space with another design firm, and the owner interviewed an applicant and thought she was really sweet and talented. She sent a thank-you letter and spelled his name wrong. That was it for her. How do you know that somebody is going to check the client's work correctly? We are creating design that communicates. We are not just creating pretty stuff. If we are setting a capabilities brochure for a Fortune 500 company and we're not checking to make sure, we're not doing our job. If the client misspells something in their copy, maybe you catch it, maybe you don't. But if you had to typeset a correction, or if the job required revision, you'd better spell it right. You'd better check it, twice, before you send it back to them. As designers, we've got to be incredibly anal about attention to detail. We are not doing our job if we're not. It's a pain in the neck, but it's just part of the gig. Attention to detail, when you're somebody new and untried, is even more important. You've got to be really accurate. If you need to have somebody else proof your letter and help you set up a template, do that. Handle the simple things. So, you want a beautiful résumé, a great cover letter (spelled properly), a beautifully presented portfolio with fewer pieces that are the best of the best.

On a recent Wednesday, a young designer came by, just out of school. She had put together a little booklet on her Epson. It was just big enough to hold a mini CD. The mini CD had the whole portfolio on it in a little pocket that was hand-cut and glued up in the back. It maybe had eight pages in it with little prints of work. It was adorable. It was a fresh palette, fresh stripes across the top in bright pastels. It was very feminine, but not overly so. It was fresh, crisp. It was creative, it was cute, and the work in it was nice. It was maybe three logos, two Web pages, and a couple of CD covers. That was it. But it was a little leave-behind that was memorable.

So leave-behinds can be very effective. The portfolio is going to go away when you leave, but with any luck, your card is not going to go away. If it's a beautifully designed card, and if you are gluing it together from an Epson print, just make sure that it's printed carefully and that you cut it straight. Again, that demonstrates your hand skills, your attention to detail.

Hand skills really are important because when you are making a presentation to a client and you've got to take boards in (because a lot of clients don't look at your first round on PDF, they want to see boards), if you're not aligning the work square on the boards, then somebody has to stand over you and make sure you're doing it properly. It's sad to say, but if the artwork is crooked on a board it takes away from the impression of the work itself.

I guess it comes down to a sense of personal pride. If you cut your card out nicely, and you've assembled a great leave-behind, and it's well done, that speaks well about you. When you go to an interview, maybe don't wear all the rings (if you usually do, of course!). Don't go to an interview—unless you're going to a grunge-film studio—in a torn T-shirt and jeans. Have a little respect for the people that you are seeing. Casual is fine. You don't need to show up in a suit and tie—that would be ridiculous. No sports coats, please. You're a designer, for goodness sake. But have clean pants and a clean shirt. Look cool. Look hip. You're in a profession where we know you will sweat and slave and you'll work twenty-four hours straight sometimes, and you'll wonder what the hell you ever were doing even getting in here. But still, you're in something the public perceives as being very cool. So dress the part. Have fun, smile, be courteous—the things your grandmother told you to do. Those all apply in the business world. We're no different than a corporate client, in this respect, because—remember—we've got to take you to the client at some point, unless you are going to hide in the studio.

You've got to be able to behave like a grownup when you're going to meet the CFO of some hoity-toity corporation. Maybe he or she isn't fit to kiss your shoes, but you have to be able to pretend!

◆ ○ ◆ ▢ ◆ ○ ◆ ▢ ◆ ○ ◆ ▢ ◆ ○ ◆ ▢ ◆ ○ ◆ ▢ ◆

NAME: David Tull
JOB TITLE: Co-Creative Director/Chief Marketing Strategist
COMPANY DESCRIPTION: Advertising Agency
DEGREE: Organizational Theory and Communication Design, MFA Studio Painting
PREVIOUS JOB TITLE(S): Senior Art Director, Associated Creative Director, President and Creative Director, Chief Creative Officer
YEARS EMPLOYED IN THE DESIGN INDUSTRY: 38

Q: *How old were you when you knew you wanted to go into the arts?*
A: Pretty much since birth.

Q: *Was there a particular event or person that inspired you to become an artist?*
A: It was my natural instinct.

Q: *Where do you place notices for employment?*
A: Through the Art Director's Club and AIGA. Sometimes we do the newspaper, but we pass out a lot of our stuff to colleges around the area. We post on their public information boards. What I have found, and it's pretty annoying from an employer standpoint, is that a lot of students who are graduating have a diploma but they don't have the creative, conceptual ability. That's been my biggest disappointment in the last three or four years with hiring new employees. They have the degree, but they don't have the eye.

I had a young man in here about a month ago that had his master's degree. I swear to God, I don't know how he achieved it. I am clueless about that.

Q: *On average, how many applications do you receive for listed positions?*
A: It varies. I've got one out there now for an assistant AE, Account Executive, and I haven't heard from anybody. It's been up there about a month. Art director is probably the most prevalent of the occupations that people respond to. Then again, when they come in and show their portfolio, I'll give somebody an opportunity if it looks like they can pull it off. I haven't seen a lot of them that can pull it off. We have what we call a three-month grace period. If you don't fit those certain expectations in those three months, it doesn't pay for us to keep you onboard. A lot of people have not been able to fill that time of three months, and to show us any diligence, and that they have the creative ability to do it.

Q: *Do you begin notifying people that they may be considered for an interview as soon as you review applications?*
A: Absolutely.

Q: *If there is an applicant that doesn't have every skill listed as required in the job description, should they still apply?*
A: It would be a waste of their time and our time. I am really specific about time management and if you don't have it, don't apply. If you can give me a song and dance about a spectacular portfolio, perhaps I'll talk to you.

Q: *If a job ad says that an applicant should know five programs and they only have experience with four out of the five, he or she shouldn't bother applying?*
A: If they have a general idea about number five, come on in.

Q: *How much do you value the experience gained in internships?*
A: I value it a lot. That can make or break a business opportunity or an appointment opportunity.

Q: *Is it possible for new graduates to get a job in a position that is more than intern or entry level?*
A: Not from what I have seen lately. I have really been disappointed in the quality of creativity that's coming from students today. I don't blame that on students, I blame that on faculty and staff for not giving the proper direction and encouraging them to do some things instead of other things. It's not the student's fault.

Q: *Is more attention given to artists with master's degrees?*
A: No. It's nice to have, but no.

Q: *Is experience preferred over education?*
A: Absolutely.

Q: *Should a résumé fit on one page?*
A: Preferably. Unless they're my age. Mine is about four pages long. Try to minimize it down to one page.

Q: *Do you prefer a short, highlight-oriented résumé or something that provides a more detailed description of past work experience?*
A: Short, and you can explain it when you get here.

Q: *Should a person applying for a graphic design job design his or her résumé?*
A: What I have found to be a real turnoff are résumés on which an applicant designs his or her own logo and doesn't use typography

properly. That's a big turnoff for a creative director. If they are oriented in design, and have a good eye, and good balance, and they know typography, bring it on. But if you don't, that's like bull-shitting me.

Q: *When reviewing work samples, do you look for designs that resemble work you have done in the past, or do you look for eye-catching work of any sort?*
A: I want something fresh, unique, and different. Anybody can duplicate a Milton Glazer or Seymour Chwast. I don't want to see something that's been done all over again. I just want to see something new and refreshing.

Q: *When submitting work samples, is it important to display a range of work, such as logo, page layout, and poster design?*
A: Absolutely. It shows your versatility.

Q: *So if an applicant had to submit three samples, he or she should send one of each?*
A: One of three different things, yes.

Q: *Do you prefer work submitted by regular mail or e-mail?*
A: I prefer by regular mail, personally. I like to hold it in my hand. Even though I can print a hard copy, I like to hold it in my hand. I like to see how they put that thing on the page.

Q: *Is it necessary for a graphic designer to have good print production skills?*
A: Yes.

Q: *What is the purpose of a cover letter and what are you looking for in it?*
A: A cover letter to me is more or less like a pre-introduction to your skills and where you're coming from.

Q: *Do you know when you are reading a generic cover letter?*
A: Oh sure. I've been through a million of them.

Q: *If an applicant sends a generic cover letter, does that hurt his or her chances?*
A: Normally, if they have an e-mail address, I'll e-mail them a note saying, "Thank you very much, but no thanks."

Q: *About what percentage of people get called in for interviews?*
A: About three percent.

Q: *What characteristics do you look for in someone you are interviewing?*
A: They have to be open, friendly, honest, and look me straight in the eyes.

Q: *If you interview an applicant and you like him and his work, do you let him know right away or is there a waiting period involved?*
A: If I find that his work isn't up to what we're looking for, I let him know immediately. That way he can move on.

Q: *What kind of creative skills do you look for?*
A: You have to have a good eye. You have to have a good mind. You have to be able to spell. I'd like you to have a conceptual ability with color.

Q: *How many people are applicants interviewed by when they come in?*
A: The other co-creative director and my senior art director; there are three.

Q: *Is appearance important?*
A: Absolutely, because sometimes you deal directly with a client. So it's everything sometimes.

Q: *Does it hamper an artist's ability to be hired if their appearance doesn't smatch that of a typical professional?*
A: It depends on if they are going to hang out in the back of the house, or if they are going to be in the back and front of the house. It depends on your position. Our designer is not necessarily spiffy all the time. Our senior art director is. Anybody that deals with a client should have some sense of dressing. Dress appropriately.

Q: *Do you ask questions designed to catch people off guard?*
A: Not intentionally. I ask them basic marketing, advertising, and design questions that they should be aware of and know of. I don't try to push anybody into a corner.

Q: *Do you use freelancers?*
A: Yes, we do.

Q: *Where do you find freelancers?*
A: A lot of times they come from interviews, situations where we just can't hire them on a full-time basis.

Q: *Do you welcome submissions from people that are looking to do freelance work?*
A: Absolutely.

Q: *How did your last or current designer get his or her position?*
A: By word of mouth.

Q: *Do you have any other suggestions for artists who are seeking employment?*
A: Have a rounded knowledge of advertising, marketing, design, and a gut feeling for design.

Q: *Is it important to have an understanding of the business side of things?*
A: Absolutely. Financial acumen never hurt anyone.

◆ ○ ◆ ❑ ◆ ○ ◆ ❑ ◆ ○ ◆ ❑ ◆ ○ ◆ ❑ ◆ ○ ◆ ❑ ◆

NAME: Adam Gezelle
JOB TITLE: Senior Creative Agent
COMPANY DESCRIPTION: International Placement Agency
DEGREE: Graphic Design
PREVIOUS JOB TITLE(S): Freelance Designer
YEARS EMPLOYED IN THE DESIGN INDUSTRY: 6

Q: *How old were you when you knew you wanted to go into the arts?*
A: I was in the third grade.

Q: *Was there a particular event or person that inspired you to become an artist?*
A: I was in third grade. My teacher was punishing me. She had me sitting in the corner for a few days. During the course of my punishment, my teacher became ill and was unable to come to school. Our sub was Mrs. Tylec, and she was the art teacher. When she asked me why I was in the corner I told her I was "on punishment." She told me as long as she was the teacher she wanted me to join in with the class, and I did just that. We proceeded to have a day filled with art exercises. That day I did an illustration of two aliens holding hands. It was called "Far-Out Friends" and it won first place in a large art contest for the metropolitan area. I felt good about myself and it was a huge experience at a very early and pivotal age.

Q: *What would you say are the benefits of working with a temp agency?*
A: One of the biggest benefits is flexible hours. It's good for people who have their own home studios who just want to keep busy that little bit extra, if there is some lag time between their personal

clients. It's also a really good way, if you are new to an area, to hone in and find out what type of environments and companies use temp services. A lot of junior designers like it too because there is plenty of work out there. Companies might be looking for someone to come in and do comping and cutting matte board and that kind of thing, and they might not run an ad for it. There is a need for that type of thing. That's a good way for a junior designer to get a foot in the door and find out more about a company and see if they are still interested in pursuing what they went to school for. You have a lot of folks who are designers, graphic designers or Web designers who might come out of a four-year institution and when they get out and land their first job they become kind of disinterested. They find out it's a lot of just production, and they are not getting that conceptual role that every designer really has a passion for. That's what makes us creative people. There are various reasons that people like to do freelance and temporary work.

Q: *What is your screening process for applicants?*
A: Our screening process is a simple chain. You would submit a résumé via e-mail to us. Once that's done, if we feel that we could be an asset to you and you to us, we would bring you in. We have tests that we give individuals, we review portfolios, have them fill out all the proper paperwork, applications, I9, W4. Then, after we find out a little bit about them, and they us, we send them to appropriate positions depending on the match.

Q: *What items are required when applying to a temp agency?*
A: Nowadays we only take e-mails. We don't take faxes, we don't take walk-ins. E-mails, like a few PDF samples. Sometimes we take résumés alone. A lot of times nowadays we find that designers will have a PDF version or Word document of a résumé with a hyperlink of a Web site. That's helpful, a Web site or online portfolio.

Q: *Would you say that the process is not as formal as applying to a studio?*
A: It's not as formal. We do follow a lot of the same criteria. We don't take everyone that sends their résumé. We have to see something of value so we can give something of value to the clients that we send these folks to.

Q: *Do you work with people of all levels of experience?*
A: We do. We tend to shy away from folks who call us and say that they are "interested" in graphic design. We like to work with people who have either three to five years' professional experience or are coming out of a four-year intensive program in visual communications. I think that's an indicator to us that this person studied it formally, has gotten a formal education for X amount of years, either if it's an associate's or a B.A. or B.S. We do work with all levels—junior designers all the way up to the most senior creative art director. So, yeah, everything in between.

Q: *When applying, should applicants design their résumé?*
A: I like that. I don't like overly designed résumés. I don't need flowers and graphics on résumés. I tend to be more interested when I'm opening a PDF of a résumé that has some selective typography usage. When you're looking at thirty to forty résumés in a given week it's nice to have something stand out. I look at where someone might have worked, and where they went to school, and, of course, typos and things like that. A nicely designed résumé is refreshing to see: one with good typography and layout choices, one that uses graphic design fundamentals. I want to see spatial balance. Sometimes people will just throw words on a page. I want to see a well-laid-out résumé.

Q: *What do you look for in work samples?*
A: Just using basic, fundamental design principles.

Q: *Should applicants send different types of work?*
A: I like a variety. If they're pretty much a print person, then maybe an annual report. I like things that might look dry but have heavy text. A lot of given information, maybe something that contains charts and graphs done in Illustrator. That demonstrates to me that this person can take a bunch of information and lay it out. That's really the role of a graphic designer. Those pieces, like annual reports and newsletters, tend to be one color, two color, they are kind of dry, they're not flashy or anything. Those are things that I like to see because it's really intensive with flowing text and everything.

Q: *What characteristics do you look for in someone you have on staff?*
A: Before we would consider someone to be one of our external talents, we look for personality fit, work, work ethic, a willingness to work. When folks come in and meet with us, it's not like a formal interview where I shake their hand and let them know, "Hey, you have the job." It's a relationship where we work together. To make the relationship work, people should keep me up to date on their availability. I might interview someone on the fifteenth of a given month and they might not call me until the sixth of the following month. That to me doesn't fly. If you're going to do that, I like it when people give me a heads up. Maybe say, "I'm going through another agency," or, "I'm going to be out of town." Once they come in and we put them on the availability list, I like them to check in with me maybe once every two weeks. Drop me an e-mail or call me. That way it puts the ball in my court for me to get them out working. I will certainly call folks before I send their résumé anywhere or run questions by them about certain opportunities. I do my part and I encourage anyone that I interview to check in with me.

Q: *When a job comes in, does the agency decide who gets assigned to it?*
A: Yes. We assign work based on a variety of different questions that we ask the talent. For instance, we have to ask about their work status, their availability. Some folks are only available in the evening; some people can't work on certain days, maybe because they're taking classes or because they have a studio. We also make the match based on aesthetics. We hone in on specific skills.

Q: *When someone is assigned to a temp job, are they put through an interview process by the employer as well?*
A: Mostly, for freelance work, no. We have a really good rapport with most of the clients we work with and over the years we have sent them enough qualified candidates so it doesn't really warrant an additional interview. They want to see a résumé just so they know who this person coming through the door is and maybe a sample or two. If there is an open position that they might be thinking long-term, they might do a working interview. We do set up direct-hire interviews; that's a whole different process.

Q: *What is the difference between temporary placement and direct hire?*
A: Temporary placement is if a client calls us today and they need someone tomorrow, or they need someone next week for a month. We also do what they call in the industry a "blind temp-to-perm." That's when we don't know, and sometimes the client doesn't know, that they really need a given position filled, but they are looking for temporary help. If the person works out and the person likes it, being the talent, and the client likes the person, then a lot of times they'll be extended on their assignment, and then a lot of times they will offer the person a full-time position.

Direct hire is when a client calls us and says, "We are looking to hire someone before the summer's over, or in the next month. We had someone leave," or "We're going to open a new branch in the creative department and we need X, Y, and Z." Based on the criteria they give us, we start to send them résumés and samples of some of the designers we have if that's what they're looking for. Then there's an interviewing process. It could be a two-tier process, it could be a three-tier process, where they're going there two or three times and meeting with various folks from the creative department.

Q: *If two people have a similar skill set, how do you decide which temp person gets the assignment?*

A: It's not up to us to decide. I don't ever like to send a client too many résumés for a given position. They are paying for a service that we provide as industry experts. If they were to call and say, "We need a junior designer," I might have twenty-five junior designers. While I want them to choose, there is usually specific criteria to allow me to make a pick of twenty people and I could weed it down, typically to five people. It's usually up to the discretion of the client from there. If I send them five people, they have to pick out of the five. If they ask me, "Who do you really think?" I would say, "They are all good," or, "This person might be a little bit better for your company mission, and this person is really interested in the work you do, not just in a paycheck." There are so many variables that it's really hard to say unless you have a given scenario or specific case.

Q: *Is there something that people on the temp agency roster can do to set themselves apart and get jobs faster?*

A: I see certain things in people that make me want to get that person work. Like I said, you could have Person A, who is very talented, and Person B, who is very talented. Person A might be talented and knows they have talent and they come through the door, go through the interview process, and maybe won't call here for a month. Person B might not be as talented, but there's that level of commitment, and there's a level of integrity, and there's enthusiasm, and they understand the process, and they understand the market, and they understand that we're here to help them. We need them to help us so that we can help them. When I hear from a person and they check in, or if they tell me, "I'm going to be out of the country for a month," that's fine. I appreciate that because it makes me feel more involved in the process. It's a two-way street.

Q: *What would you say is the percentage of people who obtain full-time employment after providing temp services?*
A: Full-time employment . . . I'd like to say ninety-eight percent or something crazy like that. I don't know percentage-wise. We are pretty picky about who we bring in because we don't like to have folks come in and then sit idle for days and weeks at a time. We try to judge the market and see if it's a lot of activity, maybe on the multimedia side of things or maybe in print production. We try to act accordingly based on those observations. We don't one week do fifty interviews and then the next week do five. We try to keep it balanced according to the market.

Q: *Do you have any final suggestions for artists who are seeking employment?*
A: Learn about places. Learn about environments. Learn about places that interest you based on your work. When I came out of school with a graphic design degree, I went after companies that I would see in various magazines. If you look at prints of annual reports, or the best-of category, you might see a local shop that's featured in there and if you like the work and you want to be a part of that, go after those kinds of companies. Some folks are happy being a graphic designer anywhere. Some folks want to be a graphic designer doing a certain thing. I encourage design students that

come out of school to get involved with the industry and the creative community. Get involved with your local AIGA chapter, with your local Art Director's Club. Be involved with that. Go to meetings, subscribe, go online for online chats at the Art Director's Club. You'll start to see what's out there, and then from there it's just personal preference.

Q: *Is there anything else people should know about working with a temp agency?*

A: There could be downtime. We can't always promise to keep everyone busy all of the time. It's kind of an impossibility. Even during the busiest times, it's very competitive. It's just like getting a full-time job; there's a level of competition. You have to do things that will get you over the top and get you in front of other people. The level of commitment and enthusiasm is what I look for, and it is the thing that, when I see two designers, puts one maybe a little ahead of the other. It's that willingness and wanting-ness and flexibility. There are downsides to going out as a free-lancer. You might get used to a place and really fall in love with it. But after two weeks and the assignment is done, chances are you are done there. A lot of times, clients will ask for that same person back, but it could be three months down the road.

CHAPTER 6
How to Interview Successfully

IF YOU ARE ONE OF THE PRIVILEGED FEW PEOPLE who get called in for an interview, you need to know what to expect and how to prepare. Before you have your interview, call to confirm the appointment. This will convey that you understand the practices of the business world. After you have gone through the trouble of confirming, you have to show up on time. If you don't, you will be seen as unreliable, and nobody wants that.

Every interview is worth going to. Even if for some reason you decide you don't want a job after you applied to it, you should still go. If you get called in for an interview, it means that the company you applied to thinks you have something to offer. To have any hope of performing well, you have to believe in that. You should believe that you have the talent to succeed, and it should be your goal to convince the interviewer of that. Every job interview you attend will make you more comfortable when dealing with people in positions of power.

The Job Application

Even though you submit your résumé and work samples, many potential employers require that you fill out a job application. This application asks for a lot of the same information that is on a résumé, but it also asks for more detail. It is used by the human resources department for various purposes. An application is typically two to four pages long and requires an average of fifteen minutes to complete.

These applications ask for a lot of information. You have to fill in your personal contact information. This includes name, address, birth date, phone number, e-mail address, and social security number. You have to fill in your education history. This section asks for the name and address of your high school, college, and any other institution you have attended. You also need to know the dates you were enrolled at those institutions. Some applications also ask that you provide your GPA. Another section on these long applications is your employment history. This section asks for detailed information about the last three jobs you have held. To complete this section, you must provide the name of the companies you worked for and their addresses, the name of your supervisors and their contact information, your starting salary, your ending salary, and the dates you were employed. You are also asked to provide a brief summary of what your duties were while you held those positions.

It is a great idea to be prepared to fill out one of these applications. If you arrive ten minutes early and rush to complete this application before your scheduled interview time, you will make mistakes. These applications are filled out with a pen, making your errors obvious to everyone who sees them. Making a mistake can reflect poorly on you, especially since you are applying to a position that requires an attention to detail. To be prepared, write out all of the necessary information on a sheet of paper and bring it with you. Copying information is much easier than recalling it from memory.

You should call the company and ask if you will have to fill out an application before your interview. If so, arrive twenty minutes early. That should give you enough time to complete the application without having a panic attack. Whether or not you have an application to complete, you should always arrive at least ten minutes early.

What to Bring with You

Obviously, the most important thing to bring is your portfolio. The majority agrees that you should include around ten of your best pieces if you have ten. Nobody wants to see a portfolio of seventy-plus pieces. It is not impressive to anyone if your portfolio weighs fifty pounds. As most of my interviewees have said, repeatedly, if you only have three strong pieces, only include those three. You are trying to make the best impression possible.

Put your strongest pieces in the front and the back. It is a proven psychological fact that when people are viewing a sequence of items they remember the first and the last the best. When they are thinking about you after you leave, you want your best work to linger in their minds. You should also show respect for your work. It should be clear that you care about the work in your portfolio. Bring an extra copy of your résumé along with a leave-behind.

As I've said before, a leave-behind is something small that you can give to the person who interviews you. You can't leave your entire portfolio, so this is a small sample of your work that will be there after you have left. It could be something as simple as a business card. Some people go so far as to create a CD package and put their portfolio on the CD. Other people choose to create a booklet that has small prints inside. Every time they see that item, they will think about you and your work.

Communication Is Essential

When you show up for the interview, be personable. Verbal communication skills are essential for a designer. You have to be able to explain why you did what you did with your work. If you receive some constructive criticism, catching an attitude is not the proper response. More than likely, a recent graduate will be interviewing for an entry-level position. You have to realize that you don't know everything there is to know about design. People who have been in the business for fifty years are still learning new things. You should have the attitude of a person who knows they have a lot to learn.

At the same time, you should be confident about your work. Don't apologize for anything. Potential employers want to see that you know you are capable of creating professional-quality designs. When you are asked to show your work, you should present it in a professional manner. If you do a good job with the presentation, you will instantly be seen as an effective communicator who understands the principles of design.

The presentation will probably be familiar to anyone who has gone through formal design school training. Presentations during a job interview are no different, except there is a job on the line instead of a grade. You would begin by taking out a single piece of work and showing it to the employer. You could just put it on the table in front of him or her if it is a one-on-one interview. If many people are present, you might want to stand at the head of the conference table and prop your work up on an easel (or improvise with a typing stand). After you let the viewers see the work, explain to them what the design problem was that you were trying to solve, the creative process that led you to the solution, and how the elements of your design solve the problem, in terms of concept, space, type, color, and shape. After that, respond to any criticisms they might have of the piece. Of course, you have to be clued into the interpersonal tone of the interview. If it doesn't seem like the interviewers are looking for a long, formal presentations, scale it back.

When the interviewers are talking to you, make sure you are respectfully listening to everything they say. They will ask you about yourself and you have to be prepared to answer those questions. They may ask why you want to work for them, why you decided to become a designer, or other questions that give them a better idea of who you are as a person. The following is a list of questions you may be asked. Each question is followed by a brief explanation of the kind of answer you should give.

* *What is the most difficult design challenge you have faced and how did you solve it?*

> Think back to a difficult design problem that forced you to reach into the very depths of your mind. Describe that problem and the process you went through to solve it. There is nothing wrong with admitting that something was difficult as long as you were able to resolve it. If you are the kind of designer that creates everything in twenty minutes, make something up. The interviewer may see you as arrogant and dismissive if you say something like, "Difficult? All designers should study my work."

* *What do you enjoy most about designing?*

> Be honest. Whether you know it or not, there is a reason you chose design as your profession. If you made that

choice, there must be something about it that you enjoy. Talk about that reason as openly as possible.

* *What do you dislike most about designing?*

You probably shouldn't be completely honest about this question. Don't say "dumbass projects," no matter how bad you might want to. Try to find an answer that makes you look like a good worker. Something like "The day I have to turn it in" would be a good answer. The explanation to that would be you are very critical of your work and believe that everything can be made better even if given ten extra minutes to work on it.

* *Where do you see yourself in five years?*

I rarely know where I will be tomorrow. I hate that question. The interviewer wants to hear that you will be with their company, learning and growing as an employee. So tell them that.

* *What salary were you expecting?*

Give a range of numbers. The size of that range is up to you. We would all like to make six figures, but be realistic. Look around at job listings to find a reasonable range of numbers and respond with that. It also helps to mention that the salary you want is a flexible figure.

* *What type of projects do you most enjoy working on?*

Answer this question however you have to in order to make yourself look good. If you enjoy designing CD packages and you are applying to a real estate magazine, it's better to say "Designing for magazines." If you don't want to get specific, say something like "Projects that stimulate my creativity. I love a challenge."

* *Why did you leave your last position?*

This question will explode on you if you let it. I know of several instances in which this question alone cost somebody a job. My aunt was interviewing for a job and she responded, "My boss was a (graphic language)." She spoke to her interviewer later and he told her that she would have gotten the job if not for that response. He didn't hire her because he was afraid she would talk about the people at his company in the same unflattering way. Be safe and say something to the effect of "I was looking to advance in my career and I was unable to do that in my last position." Do keep in mind that if you give your interviewer your last supervisor's phone number, he or she may double-check your response.

* *How did your educational experience prepare you to be able to fill this position?*

Recent graduates in particular should expect this question. Talk about all of the classes you took that have added to your design skills. Most schools make students go through a year of foundation before actual design classes begin. Mention the good that learning the foundation of color and balance did for you. Also mention taking classes like typography, visual communications, etc. Try to talk about any class that involved using the skills necessary to fill the job you are applying to.

* *What sort of job are you looking for?*

Saying "A job like this" is a fine answer. Describe the job you are applying to. Don't read back the job description, but in general describe something that is close it. Mention some of your career goals. If you want a job that will allow you to move into a position with more responsibilities, mention that. If there was no detailed description available when you applied, hopefully you know something about the job and the company. For example, if you know that designers at that company work on numerous projects for numerous clients, say that you like working in an environment where the projects and clients are diverse. Your answer should directly relate to the job you are applying to.

* *What sort of work are you looking to do?*

The interviewer is looking for something along the lines of "Projects that allow me to fully exercise my design abilities." If you want to be more specific and you are applying to a job that requires you to do design print projects, mention that you like designing printed material.

* *Is designing one of your strongest abilities?*

Saying no is just as bad as slapping the interviewer. If you say no, just get up and leave. Saying yes is a must here. After you say yes, describe your creative process and some of the good you have been able to do with your creative thinking.

* *Who are your favorite designers?*

I know a lot of people who would not be able to answer this question, even after taking a history of graphic design class. In the case that this comes up, try to have an answer. If you don't know any names, find the names of some designers who do work you like.

* *Why do you want to work for us?*

    Kiss all the butt you can find. If you sent a cover letter, try to repeat some of its contents in your answer. Run off every fact about the company that you found in your pre-interview research. Try phrases like "I was impressed by the quality of the work in your portfolio and wanted to be part of a team of creative professionals." Again, kiss butt.

* *Why did you apply to this position?*

    Reiterate that the company is the greatest thing in the country. You should also use this as a chance to sell yourself. Tell the interviewer that you would be a good match for the position and outline the credentials you have to back up those claims.

* *If you had to describe yourself as an employee using three words, what would those three words be?*

    When asked this question, try to use a little creativity. Go through a thesaurus if you have to. After some research, it seems that the most common answers are "dependable, hard-working, and dedicated." Try to say something else. Your potential employer wants to hear adjectives that describe the ideal employee. Using words that the last interviewee didn't will make you stand out. There are other qualities, such as sociability, willingness to learn, and problem-solving skills, that make a potential employee appealing. Be sure to give a short explanation of why you chose each of the words or phrases that you believe define you.

Close to the end of the interview, interviewers like to hear the questions you have for them. This is another area where research is important. You should know about the company before you interview.

Don't ask questions about stuff you should know. Asking something like "So what do you guys do?" will only land you a spot in the unemployment line. Instead, ask questions like:

* *What types of projects will I handle?*

* *When a project comes in, how do you decide which designer will get the assignment?*

* *What will my responsibilities be?*

* *Will I have client contact?*

* *How are the files organized?*

* *How do you keep track of time on projects?*

* *Who will I be reporting to?*

* *How much will I be interacting with other people on staff?*

* *What are the normal hours?*

* *What is the company culture like?*

* *What opportunities are there for growth?*

* *Do you participate in conferences, competitions, and industry events?*

Many of the above questions were taken from an article by Howard Levy titled, *How to Land a Creative Job*. Asking intelligent questions will make you seem like a person who wants to do the best job possible.

It is important to be friendly because creative teams are often made of three to ten people. Ideally, those people should like each other and want to help each other do great work for clients.

Sometimes on interviews, an applicant will have to meet with more than one person. Call before the interview and ask how many people you will be seeing. Bring enough résumés and leave-behinds for all of them so nobody feels left out.

Interview Attire

Dressing for an interview doesn't require a suit and tie. You should definitely be clean, and if you have enough piercings in your face to scare animals, you should probably take a few of those out. If you follow all of the suggestions listed above, you will establish yourself as a memorable interviewee.

The Thank-You Letter

Sending a thank-you letter is one of the most important parts of an interview, even though it is done after the interview is over. An interviewer will not ask you for a thank-you letter, but will expect you to send one. People who get jobs send thank-you letters. A woman who interviewed more than twenty people for a position said that she received thank-you letters from the strongest applicants. Those applicants had carefully designed portfolios, they performed well in their interviews, and they sent thank-you letters. The strongest applicants have studied the practices of business and become strong because they know what steps to take to impress interviewers. One of those steps is sending a thank-you letter.

A thank-you letter should express your gratitude to the person you interviewed with, but it also serves another purpose. Without restating your entire history, you can summarize the reasons why you should be chosen to fill the position. Your thank-you letter, like your résumé and cover letter, should be one page long.

Like a cover letter, a thank-you letter should be written on the same letterhead as your résumé. At the top, write your name and address. Under your address, write the date. Under the date, write the name of the person who interviewed you, his job title, and his address. Make absolutely sure you spell the name right. If you don't, no matter how flattering your thank-you letter is, it will never be read and you won't get hired. Spelling something as simple as a name wrong is a really shameful way to lose a job. The first line in the text of the body should read "Dear (whoever interviewed you)."

In the first paragraph of the letter, express how truly grateful you were to have met with the person who took time out of his schedule to consider making you a part of the staff. The first sentence could read, "I would like to thank you for taking time out of your schedule to meet with me to discuss the graphic designer position at (XYZ Company)." After the interview, you should have more information about the position. Use that to your advantage. Write something along the lines of, "Now that I have learned more about the position, I am even more interested in working for you." If there is something about the job that you find particularly appealing, mention that too. After you state how thankful you are and the fact that you want to work for the company really badly, you get to talk about yourself a little.

The second paragraph of your letter should summarize the skills and experience you have that would allow you to succeed at the position you are applying for. This is an opportunity to remind the employer of why he should hire you. You should state your strongest characteristic, and other aspects of your background that would allow you to perform more effectively than the other applicants. This paragraph should read something like: "I believe the skills and experience I possess match the requirements you are look-ing for in a designer. Along with my passion for design, I would bring my knowledge of multimedia and illustration to this position." (I do not recommend that you copy these examples word for word.)

The third and final paragraph should tell the employer that you are available to answer any follow-up questions he may have. It should also be made clear that you would be open to having a sec-ond meeting and that you are looking forward to hearing from him. In closing, thank the employer for considering you for the position. Close the letter with "Sincerely," your handwritten signature, and your name printed below.

Thank-you letters should be sent the same day of the interview. That way the letter has a chance of being received before a final hiring decision is made. To write a good thank-you letter, you must use information gathered in the interview. Therefore, do not give your interviewer a thank-you letter as the interview is ending. If you hand him a thank-you letter before you leave his office, he will assume that you don't want the position because that is an improper business practice. It is also another stupid way to lose a job opportu-nity. Send your thank-you letters through regular mail. That is the way people expect to receive them. Taking this extra step will force interviewers to give you serious consideration when they are making hiring decisions.

CHAPTER 7
Interview Tales

I DON'T WANT TO SOUND like an infomercial, but the suggestions in this book have helped me. The improvement in my applications for design jobs has been obvious. Before I put this book together, I applied to forty jobs during the two months that I was out of school. Of those forty, two responded and offered me interviews. That is a pathetic percentage. Due to circumstances beyond my control, I wasn't able to attend those interviews. While I was writing this book, I stopped applying for full-time work so that I could give my full attention to this project. When I finished the first draft, I started applying again.

My second application effort included applications to eight jobs. Of those eight, three responded and offered me interviews. I was a lot happier with those results. This time around I was not going to let anything stop me from attending the interviews. One of the interviews was with a very active design firm with a staff of six that does a lot of work for nonprofit organizations. It marked the first time I interviewed for a full-time design position.

Entry-Level Graphic Designer Position

The position I was being considered for was entry-level graphic designer. I found the position posted in the job section of a newspaper's Web site. The listing asked that applicants send a résumé and work samples via e-mail. I sent my résumé in Word format and two samples of my work. Two days later, I was contacted by the president of the company and instructed to call the firm to schedule an interview. After a day of phone tag, I was finally able to reach her and schedule a meeting. After scheduling the interview, I started my preparation.

I went to the firm's Web site, making sure I viewed every piece it had on display in its portfolio. I did some other research online and learned that the firm had won numerous awards. After I learned more about its reputation, I knew I wanted to be on staff. The majority of my preparation time was used to prepare my leave-behind. I had been making a lot of CDs, so I decided to create a CD package, including all of my portfolio pieces on the CD. The design of the CD cover and the CD itself was consistent with my résumé and Web site. It was done with the same kind of imagery and color palette. With my knowledge of the company and my leave-behind prepared, I was ready for the interview.

When I arrived at the office, I was shown into a conference room and instructed to take a seat. I picked a seat toward the front of the table, leaving the head seat for the president of the company who was interviewing me. She was very friendly. After exchanging pleasantries, she took out a copy of my résumé. One of the first things she told me was that the design of my résumé had gotten me the interview. Lucky for me, my résumé was one of the few in the pool of applicants that stood out. After revealing the reason that I was fortunate enough to get an interview, she asked her first question. It was a question that can be terrifying if you are not a person who likes to brag. The question was "Why are you a fantastic designer?" Bragging is something I am great at, so that was no problem. She continued to rattle off questions and I continued to field them. I was very comfortable talking to her, somebody I had just met, probably because of all the interviews I had conducted for this book. Some of her other questions were:

* *What is the most difficult design challenge you have faced and how did you solve it?*

* *What do you enjoy most about designing?*

* *What do you dislike most about designing?*

* *Where do you see yourself in five years?*

* *What salary were you expecting?*

* *Why do you want to work for us?*

* *What type of projects do you most enjoy working on?*

The salary question was something that I was prepared for. I had been vigorously looking for work over the two months preceding the interview, and through that search I discovered that thirty to forty thousand dollars is the average salary for an entry-level graphic designer. I didn't want to give them an outrageous figure. I did, however, want to be making as much money as the company was willing to pay me. I decided to answer the salary question with a range of numbers. The range I gave was the one mentioned, thirty to forty thousand. My interviewer responded with a simple "OK."

As far as I could tell, I answered all of the questions in a confident and intelligent manner. I was prepared for the type of questions that I was asked because of my research. After her questions, she said, "I would love to see some work." This, of course, was when I broke out my portfolio. As I went through the book, I explained the goals of the projects, and I also outlined my thought process for each. My portfolio, consisting of seven pieces, was presented in a leather-covered portfolio I purchased at an art store for fifty-five dollars. Four of the pieces were created during my four-year internship. The other three pieces were design projects that I created specifically to include in my portfolio. I was only satisfied with a few of the pieces I created at my internship because my design choices were limited by client restrictions. The three pieces I created specifically for my portfolio permitted me to design with no restrictions. With more freedom, I was able to create what I considered some of my best work. As I went through the portfolio, my interviewer commented that each layout was a strong piece. She gave me the impression that every piece was created and presented at a professional level. This was my first portfolio review, and I was receiving nothing but positive feedback. Based on her review, I assumed that I would be working there the next day. I was very wrong.

After the portfolio review, she asked me if I had questions for her. I whipped out a piece of paper that had my questions printed on it. The first question I asked was not on the paper. I asked for more clarification on something she mentioned earlier in the interview. The rest of the questions I asked were from the paper. I asked most, but not all, of the questions listed in chapter 6. When I was done asking my questions, the interview was over. She gave me her business card and I gave her the CD package I prepared as my leave-behind. The entire interview lasted about an hour.

I thought I had performed well throughout the interview, but after I left there were two things I wished I had done differently. The firm I was applying to does mostly print work and they were looking for a designer who was interested in doing a lot of print work. I knew that, but I didn't use that information correctly because my brain doesn't always help me. When she asked, "What type of projects do you most enjoy working on?" I replied immediately that I enjoyed working on Web projects. That was stupid. I thought that by telling her I enjoyed working on Web projects that I would illustrate the fact that I possessed many skills. I actually prefer doing print work and have only worked on a small number of Web projects. I did not express that to her clearly. I should have told her that my passion is print work and I would be ready and willing to work on Web projects if they became available.

The other aspect of the interview I wished I could have done again was to have paid better attention. The studio I interviewed in looked like an African art museum. The office I worked in for the four years before the interview was decorated with an empty cork-board and a ten-year-old scanner. When I saw all the art and statues around the office, I had a hard time looking at the woman who was asking me questions.

The interview took place on a Tuesday. I was notified on the Friday of that week that I was not going to be chosen for the position. After I received that notice, I called the woman who interviewed me and told her about the book. I asked if she would be interested in answering some questions about the interview from her perspective. She was actually excited to tell me what she thought of my performance.

When I talked to my interviewer about what she thought of me, her critiques were the same as mine. She noticed that I looked around quite a bit and didn't focus on her enough. She said that she knows the visuals in the studio are fascinating to people who see them for the first time, so she forgave me. She did mention that if I appeared distracted during an interview with someone at any other studio, I would have severely hurt my chances.

While my lack of focus didn't cost me the job, there were two reasons she gave for deciding not to hire me. The first was related to my answer about wanting to work on Web design projects. Because I mentioned that I have a fondness for doing Web work before I spoke about print work, I made her think that I was interested in finding a Web design position, not a print design position. My answer was really stupid. If you are applying to a position that requires that you design ninety-nine percent printed pieces, make sure that you say you want to design print work before you talk about any other media you enjoy working in. To discover what kind of work a position calls for, a careful reading of the job description is necessary. According to the woman who interviewed me, the other reason she passed me over was experience. Some of the other applicants that were being interviewed for the position had more experience designing for print.

On the upside, there were many things that I did correctly. She was impressed with my initial contact. The initial contact was an e-mail with my résumé and two work samples attached. She mentioned again that my résumé design got me the interview. Before I went to the interview, I asked her what the dress code was in the office. She replied "Business casual." I am no fashion expert, so I still don't know what that means. To avoid any problems, I decided to wear the classic interview outfit, a suit and tie. A few of the interviewees in this book have said that a suit and tie are not necessary, but my interviewer said I presented myself as a professional by wearing a suit. Something else she noted was my respect for my work. From my presentation she could tell that I was proud of my portfolio. That quality was something she was looking for in everybody she interviewed. Some of the other applicants she interviewed brought their work in paper bags. They did not get the job. The thank-you letter I sent served its purpose perfectly. It let her know that I appreciated the time she took to meet with me and that I really wanted to work there. I was told that my thank-you letter was one of the most articulate ones she had received.

During the whole process, from applying to sending a thank-you letter after the interview, I presented myself as a design professional, and I had a decent chance of getting the job. It seems that I was a victim of a more experienced applicant pool and some bad answer choices. Those disadvantages were too much for the well-designed work in my portfolio to overcome. From my post-interview discussion, I learned that I needed to think more before I answer questions. Talking fast may make you look confident, but if you talk too fast without thinking clearly you may talk yourself out of a job.

Layout Artist/Graphic Designer Position

The second design interview of my career was scheduled the day after my first. I was feeling confident about my performance the previous day, and I was mentally prepared when it came time to meet with my interviewer, the director of publications at a college in my area. I also found this posting in the job section of a newspaper's Web site. The title of the position was layout artist/graphic designer. The position was described as having two duties: arranging a weekly newspaper, and creating designs for projects as they were requested by other departments. I applied by sending my résumé, a cover letter, and three samples of my work as attachments in an e-mail. The samples I sent were different because I designed a piece intended to impress the reviewer of my application. I knew I was applying to a design position at a college, so I designed a cover for a student handbook. My application materials were impressive enough to prompt the college to notify me that I would be further considered for the position.

My first contact with the interviewer was in the form of a pre-interview over the phone. I was told that the pre-interview was used to weed out the applicants who were no longer interested, or not qualified. He asked questions about my educational experience and my familiarity with graphics programs. He explained the details of the position and asked if that description was something I would be interested in. I made it clear that I was anxious to receive the opportunity to do everything he described. This lasted thirty minutes, and at the end I had an appointment to meet with him in person.

In a suit and tie, I arrived for the interview twenty minutes early. I was instructed to sit in the lobby and wait for my interviewer to find me. Fifteen minutes after I sat down, the interviewer and I shook hands before going into his office. He began by giving me more details about the position. All of his questions came from a piece of paper he had in a folder. As I answered the questions, he jotted notes on my responses. It took all my energy not to look down to make sure he wasn't writing something I didn't like. Some of his questions were:

* *What was the most difficult challenge you faced at your last position?*

* *Why did you leave your last position?*

* *How did your educational experience prepare you to be able to fill this position?*

He didn't ask me about salary. The salary for the position was listed as part of the job's description on the university's Web site. He decided not to ask me two of the questions because those could only be answered by someone with "more experience." He told me that some of the people he was interviewing had a lot more experience than I did. That bothered me because it sounded like he was preparing me to hear that I wasn't going to get the job.

After his questions, he told me he wanted to see my portfolio. I brought it out and presented it in the same way I had at my first interview. The specially designed student handbook cover was the first piece in my portfolio. Much like my first interview, I received positive feedback on all of my work. The interviewer even told me that he was impressed by everything I showed him. After the presentation of the portfolio, he told me that he was open to any questions I had. Again, I was ready with my sheet of questions. One of the questions inspired him to share some of his personal feelings about the inner workings of the publications department, so I guess it was a good one. After I finished asking my questions, my interviewer decided to give me a tour of the office. This didn't include meeting any other staff members, but he did show me around the office, including a stop at the desk where I would work if I got the job. I gave him my leave-behind CD when he gave me his business card, and the interview was over.

From my perspective, I did everything correctly during the interview. Based on his reactions to my answers, I assumed he sincerely believed I was a viable candidate for the position. I was pleased with everything I had said during that interview. As part of an effort to correct the mistakes made in my first interview, I stared directly into the face of the man I was talking to. Focus was something I had trouble with in the first interview, and I wasn't going to let that detract from my performance a second time. I corrected the mistakes I made at the first interview, allowing me to conduct what I thought was a nearly flawless interview.

Two days later, I sent a thank-you letter to the man that had interviewed me, letting him know how thankful I was. Ten days later, he sent me a letter letting me know that he was still deciding on who should fill the position. I didn't want to annoy him, so

I decided that I would wait a while before I contacted him again. His e-mail said that he would notify me once a decision had been made, and I expected him to do just that. I found out later that waiting three weeks after the interview to ask about my standing for the position made me seem uninterested.

I had the chance to speak with the man who interviewed me. I called him and he graciously took time out of his schedule to tell me why he hadn't given me the job. The day we talked was about a month after the interview. He began the conversation by telling me he had given the job to somebody else. He said that I didn't do anything wrong at the interview. Some of his comments were that I was "responsive, punctual, well-dressed, and presented myself in the best way possible." That was consistent with my feelings about our meeting. He went on to say that I presented my work in a professional manner. My portfolio, according to him, was one of the best he had seen in a while. The only suggestion he made was that I should have contacted him about the job sooner than I did. All the other people he interviewed contacted him sooner, which made it clear that they still wanted the job. The lateness of my contact hurt my chances of being hired. If I had done everything right, except for asking about the job before a month had passed, I assumed that he had a good reason for not giving me the job. He offered me a logical explanation.

The horror of not having enough experience came up again. My interviewer explained that the office I would have been working in was going through a transitional period and the person filling the position would be under close scrutiny. He didn't want me, someone just starting his career, to hold a position in a semi-hostile environment. He felt that someone with more experience would be able to deal with having people analyze every move he made while at the office. The person he hired had eight years experience with publications and design. More than fifty people had applied for the position, and five of them, including me, had gotten interviews. I ended up being his second choice for the job. That made me feel nice, but it still sucked.

I had all the technical skills required for the position, I gave a flawless performance in my interview, my portfolio was better than the other applicants', and I felt comfortable around the interviewer. For those reasons, I should have gotten the job. I was passed over because I had less experience, and I applied at a time that would have made the job difficult for me. If I had applied for this position when the environment in the office was stable, I believe I would have been offered the job. Because of outside factors, having a friendly personality and a strong portfolio will not always be enough.

Web Designer Position

I never actually applied for the Web designer position. It was brought to my attention at an interview for a more boring job. I applied to be a data entry assistant through a temp agency. The listing for this job was on the same newspaper site as the other jobs I interviewed for. When I applied, my résumé was the only item I submitted. It wasn't a design position, so I didn't include any work samples. The temp agency called me in to interview for the data entry assistant position three days after I submitted my résumé.

In preparation for the interview, I visited the company's Web site to gather all the information I could. All I found out was that it was a temp agency that had three recruiters on staff. In my research I had found that doing a successful interview at a temp agency requires a clear understanding of the skill set one possesses. I practiced giving a speech about the skills I possess and the programs I am able to use proficiently. I decided to wear a suit and tie to this interview because I wanted to look professional.

When I went to the interview, I didn't need my portfolio, since the position I was interviewing for was not art related, but I did take a copy of my résumé. I arrived to the interview fifteen minutes early and was prompted to take a seat near the reception desk. Soon after I sat down my interviewer brought me a job application along with some tax forms. The job application I had to fill out was exactly like the application described in chapter 6. Because I had brought with me a printout of all the necessary information, completing the form was easy. I finished in ten minutes, providing me a few moments to relax before the interview was scheduled to start.

My interviewer's goal was to assess my ability to fill the position. He wanted to make sure that I had the skills and interest necessary to meet the needs of the client I would be working for. I was told that the temp agency made every effort possible to match the right people with the right jobs. During the interview, he asked me questions like:

* *What sort of job are you looking for?*

* *What sort of work are you looking to do?*

* *What salary range are you looking for?*

As he continued the interrogation, he began to ask about my background in design. I explained that my passion was designing, but I was anxious to fill any position I could do well. I really wanted some money, so I made it clear that I would be willing to do any job that involved a computer. The interviewer brought it to my attention that one of the companies he was recruiting for was an active Web design firm. I jumped at that opportunity and gave up on that stupid data entry job. After he mentioned the Web design opportunity, I gave him my URL, which was not included on the résumé I had submitted for the data entry position. He told me he would review the work on my

Web site to see if my portfolio was good enough to warrant a meeting with the Web design firm. Two days later my interviewer called me to let me know the Web design firm was interested in meeting with me. The president of the firm called me to arrange an interview.

The interview with the man at the Web design firm was shorter than the interview at the temp agency. It was shorter because the temp agency recruiter had relayed a lot of the information I had provided at the first interview. I did not have to fill out any paperwork because the temp agency handled all of the documentation. All I had to do was show up and answer some questions. This was for a design position, so I brought my portfolio.

The president of the Web design firm didn't ask me that many questions. He spent the majority of the time describing the position. He made it clear to me that the company was small and I would be required to perform a number of duties, because employees of small design firms have to be versatile. The position itself was a temp-to-hire position. A temp-to-hire position begins with a ninety-day trial period. Once the ninety days are over, the employee and the company decide if the relationship should continue. If the company decides to hire the employee as a permanent staff member, salary is renegotiated and usually raised.

When he was asking me questions, he wanted to know how much experience I had designing Web sites, and was also curious about my comfort level with Web-related software. One of the few questions he asked me was, "Is designing one of your strongest abilities?" I had many answers memorized, so I ran through that question with scientific precision. After he asked his two or three questions he said he was going to browse my Web site for samples of my work. I saved him the trouble and showed him my portfolio. Once my presentation was over, I pulled out my list of questions again. I wanted to get more information about the aspects of the position that he neglected to mention.

This interview was another success. Before I left, the interviewer said, "I thought that went well." I knew then that my interview technique was improving because that was the first time I had heard those words from a potential employer. Although I performed well, there was something I had neglected to do, and that was give him a leave-behind. I wasn't able to spend as much time preparing for the interview because, at that time, I was involved in many projects that needed my attention. My lack of focus on the interview caused me to forget to prepare a leave-behind to give the Web design interviewer. When I realized this, I was already in the middle of the interview. There was nothing I could do. But I didn't think the lack of a leave-behind would cost me the job—and it didn't. I was lucky in this case, because none of the other four people interviewed for the position had brought in a leave-behind either. The interviewer later said that if any of the interviewees had given him a leave-behind, he may have made a different decision. You will do yourself a great service if you lay out all of the materials you need the night before the interview, to ensure that you are properly prepared.

The large majority of job interviews are structured the same way. You are asked a bunch of questions, you show your portfolio, you ask questions, you drop off a leave-behind, and then you leave. That is why my interview style, answers, and portfolio presentation were the same for each interview. I have received favorable reviews from all of the people I interviewed with, which is why I changed very little from interview to interview. If you find an interview style and set of answers that works for you, stick to it. It will become something you are comfortable doing no matter who you are talking to.

When an interview is over, you will know if it went well or not. If you think it went well, it probably did. If you have some regrets or wish you had done something differently, the interviewer probably noticed the same mistakes you did. Don't dwell on those mistakes. It is important to remember there will be future interviews in which you will be able to correct them.

The first interviewer I met with decided to give the job to someone else, but she said she would keep me in mind in case some Web
projects came into her office. A good interview will always create
the potential for freelance work. Going to the first interview made
me better prepared for the second. At the second interview, I managed not to give any responses that made the interviewer think I was
applying to the wrong position. After the second interview, the man
I met with also told me he would consider giving me something to
work on if his office received projects they were unable to handle.
Although I did not get those two jobs, the possibility of doing freelance work was better than nothing. I was offered the job at the third
company I interviewed with, but I declined the position because
better opportunities arose. I went from getting no responses to being
offered a job designing Web pages. Once I began presenting myself
in the way expected of a design professional, I started to receive the
responses I knew I deserved.

CHAPTER 8

Evaluating and Accepting the Right Job

WHEN SEARCHING FOR A JOB in the early stages of your career, it can be difficult to know what to look for. If you have never had a job, how can you know what sort of environment your talents will be most effective in? There are a few key questions you should ask and seek the answer to when considering whether or not to accept a job.

Finding a Good Fit

Do you know what you want from a job? That is a question you should rack your mind to try to answer. Knowing what you want from a position will make finding work easier. It is important to know the type of work you want to do. If you are able to decide on an area of focus, there are benefits that go along with that decision. By dedicating yourself to one avenue of design, you will be applying to fewer jobs, but all of those jobs will be positions you desire to fill. In addition to having to submit fewer applications, concentrating on one area will allow you to develop more proficiency. If you put all of your time and effort into studying and working on movie poster design, companies that design movie posters will find you more attractive as an applicant because your level of skill will be more advanced than those competing against you. This type of career focus is for people who know what they want to do with their talents. The drawback to making this decision is that there will be fewer positions available for you to fill. A person who is dedicated to doing movie poster design may be increasing one skill at the cost of others. Studying one area may prevent you from developing new abilities.

There are also advantages to being well rounded. By deciding to learn and practice as many design areas as possible, more opportunities will be available to you. Many employers appreciate someone who is flexible enough to work in two or more disciplines. If you work for a company that only does print design, your employers won't care about your Web design skills. However, if you interview with a company that works in print and on the Web, being comfortable in both will give you an advantage over other applicants. We should all be seeking jobs that will reward us for the skills we have without having to put up with a bunch of crap. Don't settle for anything less.

With enough searching, you should be able to find a position that you won't hate showing up for. When you have a full-time job, assuming that you want to keep it, you have to show up on time every day, and stay there for at least eight hours. That number is usually even higher for creative people. If you have to put in that much time, you will be a much more pleasant person if you are comfortable in your workplace, creating work that you can be proud of.

A Job Offer Is Just the Beginning

Let's assume that you follow the suggestions in this book, get an interview, and receive an offer to start a job. Congratulations in advance. Receiving a job offer is not the end of your job search. Once an offer is presented, you have to decide if you will accept it.

Your first job is a great opportunity to build your portfolio. You will only be able to add to your portfolio if you are getting interesting and challenging projects to work on. Try as hard as possible to find out what you will be doing once you start working. Making coffee for the office doesn't help build your library of work. Artists turn their creative abilities into careers because of their passion for creating. That passion can and should lead to a fulfilling career.

Deciding on the right job to take is a process that should be given careful consideration. This is your chance to evaluate your potential employers the same way they evaluated you. Enjoy it. Let them see how they like it. Don't take too much time, though, because they will give your job to somebody else. You have to decide if the employer is a good fit for you. To make that decision, you first have to know what you want from an employer.

You should honestly evaluate what you know of the company that is interested in you. Based on the interview and everything else you know, does the company seem like one you would be happy with? Find out what the company culture is. Find out what is expected of designers. Some companies require employees to produce twenty-plus finished pieces per day. Would you be comfortable working at that pace? Every company has its own management philosophy. Some art directors will stand directly behind your shoulder while you are working. Less obnoxious people will meet with you once a day to track your progress on projects. Others will assign you something and not ask about it until it's due. Which of those management systems would you most prefer working under? Try to discover how the company you are thinking about working for is run during your interview. If it does not operate in a way that is compatible with your personality, you should consider looking for other positions. Getting information about these issues will allow you to make an educated decision about job offers.

In an interview, career counselor Judy Nylen of the Pratt Institute stated that comfort in the workplace and the quality of work produced at a firm are the factors that beginning artists should give the most consideration. She went on to explain that because you are going into an entry-level position, the salary you will be receiving is not up for much debate. An entry-level designer will not be making close to six figures; don't expect that. Being able to work in an environment that will allow you to grow as an artist is more important for you as a beginner than the amount of money you will be paid. If you get into a situation that does not stimulate your development, it will take that much longer for you to be able to reach a point in your career where you will be making a salary that will allow you to live comfortably and move out of your parents' house.

Another authority on design careers, Angie Wojak of Parsons School of Design, also suggests that there are more important things for new designers to consider than salary. In an interview, Ms. Wojak outlined a number of ways artists can make career decisions. She explained that besides looking at quality of work, a designer should also examine the titles of the jobs he or she will be given, as well as the titles of others working in the company. That will provide some indication of the growth potential a company has to offer. After some research into that, she suggests that you should ask yourself the question, "Will this company allow me to achieve the goals I have set for the next five years?" To learn more about a company, you shouldn't limit yourself to browsing its Web site. You should also search in outside sources that cover design topics. The more you know about a company, the easier it will be to decide if that is a place you want to lend your abilities to.

Any experience is good experience, which is why beginners especially should consider accepting any design-related job. Your first job will not be your last job. Too many people forget that and end up stuck somewhere they don't want to be for forty-plus years. That is a depressing way to live. The large majority of design positions do not involve a contract, so you can quit whenever you are good and ready. If you take a job and you hate it, you will at the very least get an idea of the kind of environment you do not want to work in. You will also appreciate a fulfilling position even more if you are unfortunate enough to work in a stressful environment first. Unless it is the most horrible, wretched job, where you feel your soul is stolen every day, you should be able to endure it until you find a more agreeable position. Once another company has agreed to hire you, quit the garbage job and move on. If they have clients and are making money, even a design shop filled with untalented designers has to be doing something right. You will be able to learn something by becoming a member of any company with an active design staff. Even with careful thought, it is difficult to determine whether a job will be a good fit for you. You will only be able to know for sure after you are actually working at a company.

Do not be afraid to ask questions at an interview. Interviewers will actually hold it against you if you don't. Using your best judgment, ask about everything you want to know. If the answers about the company do not match what you want from an employer, you may want to accept the job just for the experience until you can find something that is more fitting to you. The most important thing to remember about the job search process is that finding a job is not the end of the hunt. New opportunities arise everyday. A wise person once told me, "The day you start a job is the day you should start looking for another one." Don't end your search until you find employment that offers you everything you are seeking.

CHAPTER 9

Interviews with Business Owners

BUSINESS OWNERS are in the enviable position of never having to look for work again, assuming their business remains profitable. They instead have to search constantly for new clients and projects. People who start their own businesses decide to do so for numerous reasons. Some are not satisfied with their salary, others are not content to work for other people, and some like to be able to have access to their studio whenever inspiration hits. Whatever their reasons, it is clear that people who run a successful company have a solid understanding of both art and business. If they were not capable of executing on both ends, they would not have the success they are able to enjoy.

◆ ○ ◆ ❏ ◆ ○ ◆ ❏ ◆ ○ ◆ ❏ ◆ ○ ◆ ❏ ◆ ○ ◆ ❏ ◆

NAME: David Herbick

JOB TITLE: Owner

COMPANY DESCRIPTION: Publication, Magazine, Editorial Design Firm

DEGREE: Graphic Design

PREVIOUS JOB TITLE(S): Assistant Art Director, Associate Art Director, Senior Art Director, Graphics Director, Art Director, Design Director

YEARS EMPLOYED IN THE DESIGN INDUSTRY: 25

Q: *How old were you when you knew you wanted to go into the arts?*
A: Young. Around eight or nine, definitely elementary school age.

Q: *Was there a particular event or person that inspired you to become an artist?*
A: No.

Q: *What inspired you to start your own business?*
A: Tough one to answer. It was the right decision at the right time. I have been at this for almost twenty-five years. I've held staff jobs for a good seventeen, eighteen years. There are a lot of reasons why I started my own business. Some are personal. I didn't want to live and work in New York. I moved down here when I couldn't find employment back in New York that I found suitable. I didn't want to move back to the city in the end because I've got kids who like it here. It was the logical next step in my career path.

Q: *What was the time period between when you decided to start your own business and when the business was actually up and running?*
A: It wasn't that clear. It wasn't like suddenly a light bulb went off and I knew I wanted to start my own business. I was doing freelance assignments on the side. I had done publication redesign work while I was on staff. It was an evolutionary thing.

Q: *When you did freelance work, where did you go to find it?*
A: It came to me. You're talking about somebody that has been at this for a long time. The stuff that came to me came to me because I've got fifteen, twenty years of experience. They know who you are and what you're all about. It's word of mouth essentially.

Q: *What skills would you say are necessary for someone to be able to start and successfully run his or her own company?*
A: Experience.

Q: *How do you find clients?*
A: Mainly word of mouth.

Q: *What outlets do you use to advertise?*
A: I don't use any. I don't advertise in a traditional sense. But I do things like ask that I be mentioned in editor's letters in publications I have redesigned so that my name gets out.

Q: *Was it initially difficult to find clients?*
A: No, but it kept me awake at night early on thinking that this was going to be the last job I ever had. I got over that and I've been at it for five years now. The work continues to come in. I just got a big project yesterday.

Q: *Do you support yourself fully with your design business?*
A: Yes.

Q: *Do you use freelancers?*
A: Yes, on occasion.

Q: *Where do you find them?*
A: My connections here in town, knowing people, and having worked invarious places.

Q: *Do you have a roster of freelancers that you would go to if work became available?*
A: I sort of have a roster, but roster might be the wrong word because it implies there are a lot of people I go to. Mostly it's just a few people who help me out when I'm in a bind.

Q: *If you don't mind telling me, what resources did you use to find the funding necessary to start your company?*
A: I didn't. I worked out of my basement for a while. I had a set-up; I had a Mac and a scanner and all that stuff from my previous job. I had old equipment that the publication didn't want when it moved to New York. It didn't cost me much to get the business rolling.

Q: *Did you consult any professional legal or financial counselors before starting your business?*
A: I spoke to my accountant. I talked with friends who had businesses similar to what I had in mind for mine. And I spent some time reading books about launching a business. One book was really excellent: *The Business Side of Creativity*, by Cameron Foote.

◆　○　◆　▫　◆　○　◆　▫　◆　○　◆　▫　◆　○　◆　▫　◆　○　◆　▫　◆

NAME: Katie Torok
JOB TITLE: Owner
COMPANY DESCRIPTION: Design Firm
DEGREE: Graphic Design
PREVIOUS JOB TITLE(S): Graphic Designer, Senior Designer
YEARS EMPLOYED IN THE DESIGN INDUSTRY: 12

Q: *How old were you when you knew you wanted to go into the arts?*
A: One year old.

Q: *Was there a particular event or person that inspired you to become an artist?*
A: Since I have always loved drawing, the initial inspiration was from within myself, but there have been lots of people along

the way who have provided additional inspiration. The first was my grandmother. In her forties, after raising eight kids, she discovered that she was a talented artist. She always had art materials in her house, and I would just lose myself there for hours. Her name was Katie also, and I would sign all my artwork "Katie II."

Q: *What inspired you to start your own business?*
A: I knew that eventually I wanted to work for myself after getting enough experience. The real "inspiration" was when I found myself working as a designer in a studio that turned out to be a really bad environment. After a few months there, I decided that I didn't want to go back out and look for another job. It was time to start my own business.

Q: *What was the time period between when you decided to start your own business and when the business was actually up and running?*
A: It was about two weeks.

Q: *What skills would you say are necessary for someone to be able to start and successfully run his or her own company?*
A: You have to really want it. It's also important to be a great communicator, so you can sell yourself well. You also have to be resourceful and willing to delegate certain tasks to others. For example, if you are not as good at the business side, you have to be willing to find someone to help you who is. And, of course, you have to be a good designer if you are the only designer, or acting as an art director to designers you may hire.

Q: *How do you find clients?*
A: Mostly through word of mouth.

Q: *What outlets do you use to advertise?*
A: I don't really advertise in the traditional sense. Most of the work comes through word of mouth and networking.

Q: *Was it initially difficult to find clients?*
A: It was tough to get off the ground at first and I wasn't making as much as I did at my last job. Then after that, I went through two great years where work was falling into my lap. That was a period of time when the economy was great, and a lot of organizations had enough money to spend on good design. I found enough clients through networking and talking to people.

Q: *Do you support yourself fully with your design business?*
A: I am lucky enough to be married to a guy that has a really good job. And we get health insurance and other benefits through his company. But I am definitely able to take care of any household needs and feed my family.

Q: *Do you use freelancers?*
A: I have a couple designer friends who I give work to when I am really busy.

Q: *So most of the freelancers you use are people you already have a relationship with?*
A: Most of the people I give work to are people who have computers at home to work on. They are doing the same thing I am, running their own small business. They do the work at their site. A couple of times I did have to hire a temp for a few days to come in to work at my office. I have done both, but not a lot.

Q: *If you don't mind telling me, what resources did you use to find the funding necessary to start your company?*

A: I didn't get a traditional loan. We did get a loan from my husband's company, which offered an interest-free loan of up to four thousand dollars for a personal computer purchase. That was a perk from his company. Everything else went on a credit card. I initially went to the Small Business Administration. They had some workshops. They do offer loan assistance there, but I didn't go that route. Some businesses need a store and inventory and require a lot of money to start up, whereas a design business, as long as you can buy a computer, that's the big thing, and some other office things like a desk. It's not a humungous start-up compared to some other businesses.

Q: *Did you consult any professional legal or financial counselors before starting your business?*

A: I did talk to a guy at the SBA through their SCORE Association (Service Corps of Retired Executives). These are seasoned business veterans who volunteer to go in and talk one-on-one with people who have any questions about starting up a business. I did go and have a meeting with a guy there. He was pretty clueless about the design business in particular, but he did give me some good general advice about running a business. That's a good program. Also I attended a Small Business Administration workshop about starting your own business. It was either a half-day or day-long program. There were may be twenty or so people there interested in starting a variety of different businesses. They had presenters who went through the different aspects of running a business. That was helpful. Then just talking with people, designers who have done the same thing. And then networking, going to AIGA meetings and events. They put on some good business-related meetings.

Q: *Do you think that starting an independent design business is a realistic possibility for someone who has just graduated?*

A: It's possible. But I think I would really advise somebody to get a job first. There is so much you don't learn in design school. So much. My first job out of school was in a small studio. I learned more the first week than I did in all my years of school. I'm talking about the nuts and bolts of how a design studio is run. Sure, in school you learn how to be a good designer, but you generally don't learn much about dealing with clients, budgets, vendors, etc. It's certainly possible to start your own business after graduation, especially if you've had some great internships during college. But a lot of people I know who tried to do that ended up getting a job after a short period of time because they just couldn't handle the business end of things without the experience.

◆　○　◆　❑　◆　○　◆　❑　◆　○　◆　❑　◆　○　◆　❑　◆　○　◆　❑　◆

NAME: Anonymous
JOB TITLE: Owner
COMPANY DESCRIPTION: Graphic Design and Marketing
DEGREE: Communications Design
PREVIOUS JOB TITLE(S): Junior Designer, Senior Designer, Art Director, Principal
YEARS EMPLOYED IN THE DESIGN INDUSTRY: 22

Q: *How old were you when you knew you wanted to go into the arts?*
A: Junior high school age.

Q: *Was there a particular event or person that inspired you to become an artist?*
A: I always loved the arts, drawing and painting, etc.

Q: *What inspired you to start your own business?*
A: I had worked for companies for over twelve years and, at a certain point, I didn't really know what to do anymore. I just needed a change. I wasn't really always dying to have my own business. It was one of those situations where I was getting on the senior level and, unfortunately in graphic design, there's a ceiling on salaries in many parts of the business. I felt that I had a greater chance to do better if I went on my own.

Q: *What was the time period between when you decided to start your own business and when the business was actually up and running?*
A: The thing about the graphic design industry is you can be up and running when you have a job or a project. It's not a complicated business to start the way other businesses are. As far as huge investments and business plans, you really can start by getting your first project and hopefully it will snowball from there.

Q: *What skills would you say are necessary for someone to be able to start and successfully run his or her own company?*
A: It's really important to point out to graphic designers and creative people that doing the design work and running a design business are two completely different things. The first thing you have to realize is that in running a design shop, if you're lucky, you are probably going to be designing twenty-five percent of the time and doing a lot of other things the rest of the time. Often times you're so busy dealing with your clients and all the administrative parts of the business that, before you have a staff filled up, you might only get to start doing design work toward the end of the day or in the evening.

Q: *What outlets do you use to market?*
A: Targeted mailings, phone calls, and networking.

Q: *Was it initially difficult to find clients?*

A: I had some freelance clients while I was still working full time, so when I felt I had enough freelance work, I quit my job.

Q: *Do you support yourself fully with your design business?*

A: Yes.

Q: *Where do you find freelancers?*

A: That's a hard thing, because good people are hard to find. I find them through referrals, because if I have someone coming here when I'm busy, I want to know that they are not going to be a disappointment.

Q: *Have you ever used a temp agency?*

A: I did years ago, but I never was very happy with that.

Q: *What resources did you use to find the funding necessary to start your company?*

A: I started with very little. I basically had some money in the bank and bought a computer. With a few things worth about ten thousand dollars I got started. Between computer, copy machine, etc., the cost was about ten thousand dollars.

It's easy enough to get a small business started in design, but it's also easy to get into a vicious cycle of doing too much if you don't have the capital to afford helpers in the office. Having a plan is a good idea–anyone can do design from their computer, but it takes capital to grow a business.

Q: *Did you go through any business training?*

A: No, when I was in design school in the early eighties there was absolutely no business training. Design school prepared us to find our first job as designers. I don't think you need an MBA to have a design studio, but knowledge of account management, how to sell design, and good business etiquette are certainly important.

Q: *Did you consult any professional legal or financial counseling before starting your business?*
A: I talked to my accountant about whether or not to incorporate.

Q: *Do you think that starting an independent design business is a realistic possibility for someone who has just graduated?*
A: I think that that is a really bad idea. I think that it's really important to work in other people's companies to learn the business first. It's really hard to be a business owner in a field where you have absolutely no experience. Working in other people's studios you learn a lot. You learn how to be a good designer if you work under talented people.

It is common for graduates to take their bad student habits and continue making those same mistakes because they don't have a good art director to guide them. You can certainly pick up a lot of wonderful experience working in different studios.

If you can't find a full-time job, the best thing to do is just free-lance at a lot of different places. Big agency experience is a very different experience than working at a small studio where you are really working with the owner of the company. It's nice to experience a range of things.

◆ ○ ◆ ❑ ◆ ○ ◆ ❑ ◆ ○ ◆ ❑ ◆ ○ ◆ ❑ ◆ ○ ◆ ❑ ◆

NAME: Anonymous A and Anonymous B
JOB TITLE: Creative Director/Partner and Art Director/Partner
COMPANY DESCRIPTION: Graphic Design Agency
DEGREE: Graphic Design/Fine Art
PREVIOUS JOB TITLE(S): Art Director, Creative Director
YEARS EMPLOYED IN THE DESIGN INDUSTRY: 11 and 5, respectively

Q: *How old were you when you knew you wanted to go into the arts?*
A: Anonymous A: When I was about twenty-two years old.
Anonymous B: When I was about seventeen years old.

Q: *Was there a particular event or person that inspired you to become an artist?*
A: Anonymous A and Anonymous B: Not particularly. . . . we think it is something that is in your blood. You either act on it at some point in your life or you don't!

Q: *What inspired you to start your own business?*
A: Anonymous B: We really didn't like the corporate environment. It was extremely stifling creatively.

Anonymous A: When you work for a company and you do graphic design, you do sort of the same thing everyday for that particular company. You get burned out really fast. When you have your own agency, you have many different types of clients, so it seems like you're always working on something different.

Q: *What was the time period between when you decided to start your own business and when the business was actually up and running?*
A: Anonymous A: It was sort of up and running from day one only because we didn't really plan on starting our own business. There was somebody that wanted to use us for freelance work and once we started doing that, we realized how nice it was to be able to work from home on our own schedule, at midnight if we wanted to. We thought, "Hey, why can't we do this for other people too?" It kind of fell into our laps.

Q: *What skills would you say are necessary for someone to be able to start and successfully run his or her own company?*
A: Anonymous B: A "type A" personality would be first and foremost. Also strong organization.

Anonymous A: You have to know a lot about business. It's not just graphic design by any means.

Anonymous B: By no stretch of the imagination is it just design. There's a business side and a design side. If you want to do just design, don't go into business for yourself.

Q: *What is a "type A" personality?*
A: Anonymous B: I am the "type A" personality. It's crossing all the *t*s, dotting all the *i*s. Everything has to be right. This is a business where people are paying you for your taste and your "type A" personality. There's not just the art side of it, but on the back end there's the technical side, which requires the "type A." If you can do something that looks great, that's fine, but if you can't get it printed because you don't know the technical back end of everything, it's not going to work. It's all going to fall apart.

Q: *Did either of you go through any formal business training before you started?*
A: Anonymous A: No. I read a lot of books, talked to a lot of people, did a lot of research on the Internet. We tried to learn anything we could about how to get started, who to go after for business, anything that would possibly help us. We made a lot of mistakes along the way.

Q: *How do you find clients?*
A: Anonymous B: All over, for the most part. We do a lot of research into companies. Networking is probably the biggest thing. But that takes a lot of time and effort.

Anonymous A: It takes quite a while for people to really decide that they trust you and want to use your services and give you a chance. But it has been one of the best ways. It was something that we really did not want to do. Neither one of us are real outgoing, walk-up-to-people-and-meet-them kind of people. So going to huge events where you have to stand up and talk to people and talk in front of people was not our thing. But once you go often enough and you get to know these people, then they're your friends, and it's not as bad.

Q: *What outlets if any do you use to advertise?*
A: Anonymous B: A lot of what we are doing right now is word of mouth and networking. We do postcard mailings. It's pretty good for any business really just to keep fresh in everyone's mind. Whether or not they take that card and buy because of that, that's a whole different story. It's just to keep your name in people's heads.

Q: *Was it initially difficult to find clients?*
A: Anonymous B: Yeah, definitely. It's never easy. Ever.

Q: *Do you support yourself fully with your design business?*
A: Anonymous B: Yes, we do.

Q: *Do you use freelancers?*
A: Anonymous B: Yes, we do.

Q: *Where do you find them?*
A: Anonymous B: Generally, we find them at the schools where we got our bachelor degrees.

Q: *If you don't mind telling me, what resources did you use to find the funding necessary to start your company?*
A: Anonymous B: The resource was us having that "type A" personality, and savings.

Anonymous A: I was working a job that I had had for thirteen years. The last about eight of it, I was their graphic designer while

I was going to school. That was supporting the business for about the first four years. We weren't really relying on the business money for about four years. This last September, I finally made the move to go full time in the business. So since then we have been supporting ourselves with the business only.

Q: *Did you consult any professional legal or financial counselors before starting your business?*
A: Anonymous B: Not before, but as time went on, yes.

Q: *Do you think that starting an independent design business is a realistic possibility for someone who has just graduated?*
A: Anonymous B: I would have to say no just because you have to learn design first. If you're trying not only to learn how to run a business, but also how to design, you're going to make so many mistakes that you're going to lose all your clientele.

Anonymous A: There is so much that they don't teach you in school. There's so much on-the-job stuff that you have to learn that they'll never show you in school. If you do all that stuff wrong, you are never going to get clients. To get your feet wet, I think the best thing is probably to get any menial job, or something within a print company where you're just doing production and you're learning how to put together files correctly for a printer. Ultimately, if something for your client can't get printed, then you haven't done your job right. If you know how to print something, the printers love you and so does your client because there are no problems. If you know that half of it, then the next step would be trying to figure out how to get the clients.

♦ ○ ♦ ❑ ♦ ○ ♦ ❑ ♦ ○ ♦ ❑ ♦ ○ ♦ ❑ ♦ ○ ♦ ❑ ♦

NAME: Barbara Jean McAtlin
JOB TITLE: CEO
COMPANY DESCRIPTION: Graphic Design Firm

DEGREE: Studied Vocational Graphic Arts. Went straight to work in a print shop after.
PREVIOUS JOB TITLE(S): Graphic Designer
YEARS EMPLOYED IN THE DESIGN INDUSTRY: 29

Q: *How old were you when you knew you wanted to go into the arts?*
A: When I was thirteen.

Q: *Was there a particular event or person that inspired you to become an artist?*
A: I just kind of fell into the design aspect of printing after seeing it done at the places I worked. I was seeing a lot of "Look, Mom, I did it myself" jobs coming in, and because of my printing experience I was able to help the clients make their projects look cleaner and more professional. It was a real plus that I had a natural eye for design, colors, and paper, and I learned how to "know" the type of business I was working with. I've designed everything from sump-pump catalogues to adoption brochures. It's amazing what you can learn from your clients.

Q: *What inspired you to start your own business?*
A: A lousy job. I had a horrible, horrible, horrible job that I hated so bad that I thought, you know, I can do this on my own. A week after I walked out of that job I started my own business.

Q: *What skills would you say are necessary for someone to be able to start and successfully run his or her own company?*
A: Leaving your job at work when you go home. Taking time off, but still getting up and going to work in the morning. I would never be able to work out of the house. I'm not that kind of person. I have to get up and get ready for work and come into an office. It's hard to try running your own business.

Q: *How do you find clients?*
A: I actually was very fortunate that, when I walked out of my last job, I walked out with the three biggest clients my old boss had. They liked working with me, so they stayed with me. I have one of them left, and other than that it's just word of mouth. Print advertising hasn't worked for me. None of those business groups have ever worked for me. The Chamber of Commerce hasn't worked for me. It's all word of mouth.

Q: *Do you support yourself fully with your design business?*
A: Yes.

Q: *Do you use freelancers?*
A: I have once or twice.

Q: *Where do you find them?*
A: I know one guy who is awesome with Freehand computer illustration. Then another one who is also an excellent artist, architecture type of stuff. It's just getting out and meeting people. I actually ended up meeting these guys because of a hobby of mine. The hobby is Harley Davidsons. They ride and I ride. We all kind of talk together.

Q: *If you don't mind telling me, what resources did you use to find the funding necessary to start your company?*
A: Credit cards.

Q: *Did you consult any professional legal or financial counselors before starting your business?*
A: I went to a local small business development center. That gave me the information to get an EIN to keep my personal money separate from the business's money. Then I filed all the recommended paper work with the state. That was pretty much it.

Q: *Do you think that starting an independent design business is a realistic possibility for someone who has just graduated?*
A: No.

Q: *Do you have any suggestions for designers who are looking for employment?*
A: Get into the printing industry. Work in a print shop. Once you understand exactly how printing works, you will understand how to design. There are certain things that you can't do, certain things that make your design cost prohibitive for your customer and impossible for your printer.

◆　○　◆　□　◆　○　◆　□　◆　○　◆　□　◆　○　◆　□　◆　○　◆　□　◆

NAME: Howard Levy
JOB TITLE: Principal/Creative Director
COMPANY DESCRIPTION: Graphic Design Firm
DEGREE: Political Science, Creative Writing, and Journalism
PREVIOUS JOB TITLE(S): Principal and Creative Director, Art Director
YEARS EMPLOYED IN THE DESIGN INDUSTRY: 13

Q: *How old were you when you knew you wanted to go into the arts?*
A: I was creative as a child and just never stopped. I was always drawing or creating comic strips or magazines, utilizing some of the same creative and holistic skills that are essential in the design profession. Right before I started in the field, I didn't even know the field of graphic design existed, but I felt like I was bringing a combination of creative, business, and writing experience together to help clients. I still think that's a great combination that serves clients well.

Q: *Was there a particular event or person that inspired you to become an artist?*
A: When I was in college and planning my business, my friend Gabby introduced me to her father, John, who was a creative

director at the time. We struck up a friendship, and he has been a tremendous source of inspiration to me, both from the creative side and from the personal side. He is someone who has a huge amount of integrity and has provided an excellent role model in this profession. He is committed to doing work that leaves a positive impact on society. I remember him telling me about resigning from the design department of a consumer products company because their practices were deceptive. When we first met, he was co-chair of AIGA's environmentally responsible design committee, and that dove-tailed nicely with the environmental activist work I was doing on campus at the time. So essentially, he provided the bridge to believing that you could do good design work that had a positive impact on society and didn't have to compromise your values.

Q: *What inspired you to start your own business?*
A: The desire to use design as a force for positive social change. I saw there was a need to help nonprofit organizations communicate their messages more effectively.

Q: *What was the time period between when you decided to start your own business and when the business was actually up and running?*
A: Pretty much immediately. I started it out of school fourteen years ago. I was planning it while I was still in school.

Q: *What skills would you say are necessary for someone to be able to start and successfully run his or her own company?*
A: Very high talent in design, and an excellent understanding of business and what it takes to run a small business from all points of view—from identifying the right goals and potential clients to having a concerted sales effort. Also, understanding personalities and interpersonal communication skills. On the operation side, understanding

finances, bookkeeping, taxation issues, insurance and liability issues, and so forth. On the human resource side, understanding what it takes to hire, identify, nurture, train, and keep staff.

Q: *How do you find clients?*
A: Partly through networking. I have institutionalized that through starting networking groups or becoming president of various networking groups. Doing direct mail, targeted lists that we have put together on our own. I've done some advertising in some business publications. I've done a little bit of PR, sending out news releases announcing new staff appointments, or projects, or offerings that we have for different client areas. We also enter competitions.

Q: *Was it initially difficult to find clients?*
A: Yes. The biggest challenge for someone starting a business is the clients. I wouldn't recommend that you start a business unless you have enough clients to run for at least six months to a year.

Q: *Did you start your business with or without clients?*
A: I started with some clients.

Q: *Do you support yourself fully with your design business?*
A: Yes, I do.

Q: *Do you use freelancers?*
A: On rare occasion.

Q: *Where do you find them?*
A: That's a good question. When we are hiring a designer, we have a stockpile of résumés and we use that as a starting point.

Q: *What resources did you use to find the funding necessary to start your company?*
A: It was entirely self-funded from savings.

Q: *Did you talk to any professional legal or financial counselors before starting your business?*
A: Probably not, but I should have. That's an essential component to starting a business is having a good team of professionals and mentors in place.

Q: *Do you think that starting an independent design business is a realistic possibility for someone who has just graduated?*
A: I would say probably not.

Q: *Do you have any advice for designers who are currently looking for employment?*
A: I have several recommendations. Explore all possibilities—in the paper, online, job fairs, placement agencies, etc. Most of all: network. Get out there and meet people. It's tough finding a job, and you have to make a concerted effort to meet people and put your work in front of people. Most jobs are filled before they are even listed. That's motivation to meet people!

Expand your contact base by asking for informational interviews. Ask a creative director at a firm that is not hiring to review your portfolio and then ask for the name of someone else to talk to.

Join associations and attend events in the industry you want to work in—both in the creative fields and in the client industries (publishing, financial, etc.).

Look for a firm that shares your values. Young designers may look for firms that do good work so they can build their portfolios, but make sure it is a place where you would actually want to work. You will be dealing with people, so make sure your personalities are in sync. Some well-known creative firms have headstrong principals and a demanding work environment.

Research potential employers' philosophies and cultures and identify what their goals are: Do they have large retainer clients? Are they trying to win new clients? Are they trying to break into a new area? This way, you can address their needs in interviews.

It's important to understand business. Both the business side of design and the clients' business. I don't think young designers realize what is involved in selling design to clients. If you do, you'll be much more valuable, particularly with smaller firms that might have you deal directly with the client.

Focus your work and refine your abilities and portfolio in a particular area that you want to pursue. Don't be too broad in presenting things, from advertising, editorial, and package design. Employers want to see that you can think creatively, but they also want to know that you understand what their firm does and can do the work that they do. Don't take it for granted.

Learn how to present your work. By describing the assignment, you show that you understand the context and effect of your work. If you have to apologize for something in your portfolio, leave it out. And learn how to accept criticism of your work. Take it as a learning experience. Don't argue with your interviewer—they will not hire someone who cannot take criticism.

Know what kind of companies you want to go after. Research them, find out what they want, and then put together a package that reflects what their needs are.

CHAPTER 10

The Pros and Cons of Starting a Business

STARTING A BUSINESS gives you ultimate control over your design career. As the owner of a company, you decide which clients you will work with, which projects you will work on, which people you will hire, and your salary. You don't have to listen to anybody but yourself, you can take vacation when you want to, and, if your business succeeds, you will experience an incredible feeling of self-satisfaction. All of that sounds great, but operating a company that makes money is much more complicated than making business cards and calling yourself a business. There are artistic, financial, and administrative duties that must be handled if a business has any chance of succeeding.

Starting a design business doesn't require a lot of money. To start a bare-bones operation, all you need is a computer. Because there is little financial investment required, there is not much risk associated with opening a design shop. If you fail miserably, you won't be too deep in debt and you will be free to pursue other opportunities.

Starting a business is difficult for people who have been in the industry for a while, and much more difficult for an artist who is new to the industry. It's difficult for young designers because they have little experience in a studio environment and few contacts.

After talking to a number of business owners, I discovered that ninety percent of their clientele came to them by word of mouth, referral, or strength of their reputation. Recent graduates have none of these. It is possible to start a successful design business, but only if you are able to find a number of clients willing to trust a designer/owner who has little experience. That can be a lengthy process, so you will probably need other means of support while you are establishing your business.

Opening a design shop is a logical progression for people who do a lot of freelance projects. There are various legitimate forms your business could take. You could simply be a sole proprietor (you operating the business alone, and solely responsible). If you are working with someone else, you will want to set up some kind of a partnership. It might be advantageous for you to incorporate. There are liability and tax issues at stake here, so contact your attorney and accountant first.

If, against the advice of all the business owners in this book, you decide to open your own firm soon after graduation, it is important to keep in mind all of the aspects you must be willing to attend to in order to operate a business successfully. Running a business involves a lot more than creating high-quality design work. To have a profitable company, you must first establish a client base. In order to find clients, the owner of a new design firm has to actively search for them. New business owners who wait for people to come to them will be running an unprofitable company. Finding clients is made more difficult by the fact that purchasing ad space has proven to be an ineffective means of increasing a design firm's customer base. Seeking new clients is just one of the many administrative duties that a firm's principal has to manage.

When work is done for a client, somebody must bill for that work. To bill correctly, paperwork must be maintained that tracks the hours spent on the project. If work is not billed in a timely manner, it won't be paid for. If a company is not getting paid for its work, it should consider becoming a charity. Taking a class in accounting will greatly aid in the understanding of how to manage accounts. Art students are at a disadvantage in this area because most liberal arts programs don't offer classes in accounting. Even if bookkeeping or accounting is offered, most students are not taught that they might need it as part of their set of life skills somewhere down the line. Along with the bills, detailed records of the company's financial transactions must be kept for tax purposes. It takes a meticulous person who is familiar with finance to manage this information. While it is possible to gain that familiarity with experience, studying financial practices will make keeping the books that much easier.

The administrative duties of a business owner include finding new staff members and managing that staff. Managing a staff requires the ability to understand people. People are the oddest creatures walking the planet! Bringing different personalities into a small space and forcing them to work together can be the most difficult aspect of running acompany. When seeking new employees, owners take it upon themselves to find people who will fit into the company structure that has already been established. That is a huge responsibility. Hiring someone who creates chaos instead of contributing to the team can ruin a company.

Institutions like the Small Business Association have been established to assist aspiring entrepreneurs. It is the goal of these organizations to help people locate the resources and information they need to start a successful company. If you are wiling to take on all the responsibilities that business owners face on a daily basis, opening your own shop may be a better decision than working for other people.

CHAPTER 11
Résumé Gallery

MORE OFTEN THAN NOT, the résumé is the first part of an application that is reviewed. Applicants with well-designed résumés are given further consideration. Applicants with poorly assembled résumés will have their applications placed neatly in the garbage. If you want application reviewers to give you the consideration you believe you deserve, your resume must be given as much attention as any other design piece you create.

Outside the design community, the appearance of résumés tends to be uniform. Many businesses are conservative and don't encourage job seekers to employ visual flair. The following résumés were submitted by designers who were employed at the time of submission. These are the actual résumés they used in their job applications. To protect their privacy, the designers of these resumes changed their contact information before submitting to the gallery. The résumés in this gallery embody everything a designer's résumé should be. The designs, color palette (here rendered, unfortunately, only in shades of gray), and layout all work together to create design pieces that helped these designers find employment.

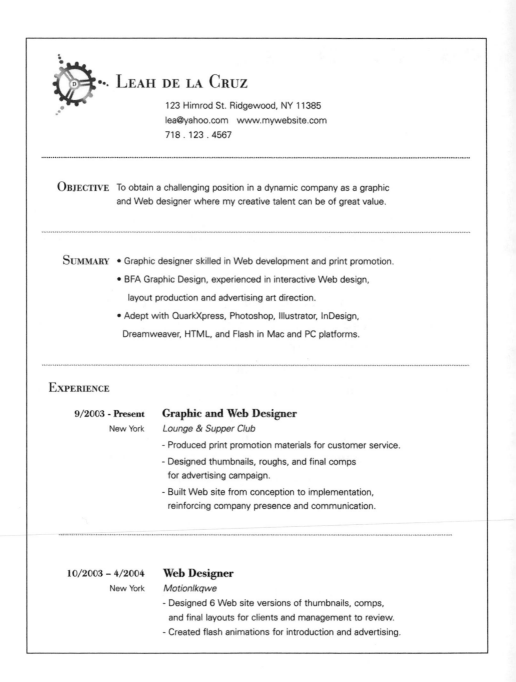

Leah de la Cruz

123 Himrod St. Ridgewood, NY 11385
lea@yahoo.com   www.mywebsite.com
718 . 123 . 4567

Objective   To obtain a challenging position in a dynamic company as a graphic
and Web designer where my creative talent can be of great value.

Summary   • Graphic designer skilled in Web development and print promotion.
• BFA Graphic Design, experienced in interactive Web design,
layout production and advertising art direction.
• Adept with QuarkXpress, Photoshop, Illustrator, InDesign,
Dreamweaver, HTML, and Flash in Mac and PC platforms.

Experience

9/2003 - Present New York	**Graphic and Web Designer** *Lounge & Supper Club*

- Produced print promotion materials for customer service.
- Designed thumbnails, roughs, and final comps
  for advertising campaign.
- Built Web site from conception to implementation,
  reinforcing company presence and communication.

10/2003 – 4/2004 New York	**Web Designer** *Motionlkqwe*

- Designed 6 Web site versions of thumbnails, comps,
  and final layouts for clients and management to review.
- Created flash animations for introduction and advertising.

EXPERIENCE

10/2003 - Present
New York

Graphic Designer
Cdsa Gourmet

- Designed and produced promotional materials including brochures, menus, business cards, posters, and banners.
- Created final layouts for press kit to strengthen company interaction with investors and clients.
- Utilized a variety of typography designed to communicate with specific audiences and support content.

2/2004 - Present
New York

Graphic and Web Designer
Qwertyui Photography Studio

- Edited and evaluated images for printing and reproduction.
- Improved Web site with stronger structures for efficiency.
- Produced layouts and compositions for photography sample books.

EDUCATION

5/2004 **Pratt Institute,** Brooklyn, NY
Bachelor's Degree - Communications Design, Graphic Design
Average GPA 3.5
Related Coursework: Illustration, Interactive Media, Art Direction, Web Design, Photography, Typography, Visual Communications

SKILLS

Photoshop	Illustrator	Pagemaker
Acrobat	InDesign	Flash
QuarkXpress	Dreamweaver	Actionscript
Imageready	HTML	PHP
Fireworks	Director	SQL
AfterEffects	Javascript	CGI

REFERENCES   Available Upon Request

Ann Jordan :: **unit_ann@hotmail.com**
415.555.1395

education ::
California College of Arts & Crafts B.F.A. Graphic Design

experience ::
Design Collective   San Francisco, California   Feb. 2000 > present
> principal contract/freelance – solely design and manage projects from inception to completion . concept and design
problem solving . organize business goals, funds and identity . maintain client contact and promote new client base .
attend client meetings . direct photo shoots . prepare mechanicals . complete press checks

Jackson Design, Inc.   Mountain View, California   Sept. 2001 > Jan. 2004
> designer – solely design and manage projects from inception to completion . concept and design problem solving .
art direct photographers, illustrators and copywriters . maintain client contact . attend client meetings . prepare
mechanicals . complete press checks

Lopez Diseño   San Francisco, California   Sept. 2001 > Sept. 2002
> intern to contractor – design and manage projects from inception to completion . art direct photographers . concept
and design problem solving . prepare mechanicals . maintain client contact . attend client meetings . aid designers
and principal . enter design competitions . office maintenance

Spartis   San Francisco, California   Sept. 2000 > Sept. 2001
> intern – assist in designing and managing projects from inception to completion . concept and design problem
solving . assist at photo shoots . prepare mechanicals . complete press checks . aid principals . maintain client contact . file and categorize book, image and portfolio library . office maintenance . enter design competitions

Lime Design   San Francisco, California   May 2000 > Sept. 2000
> intern – concept and design problem solving . assist designers and principal . file and categorize book, image and
portfolio library . office maintenance

skills ::
fluent – Adobe Illustrator CS . Adobe Photoshop CS . Quark 5.0 . Adobe InDesign CS . furniture design . screen printing
knowledge – Flash 5.0 . Dreamweaver 4.01 . Adobe After Effects 4.1

awards ::
Portal Publications judge's pick :: Poster, 2001   WADC :: Certificate of Merit, 2003
Rockport Publications :: Best of Brochures, 2003   Graphic Design :: USA Award, 2003
American Corporate Identity 20 :: 2 Logos, 2004   Logos 2004 :: Logo, 2004
HOW Self Promotion :: Stationery System, 2004   Rockport Publications :: Logos, 2004

references ::
Jake Jackson   jake@jacksondesign.com   650.555.8447
Tracy Morla   tracy@earthlink.com   415.555.0946
Luke Breidenbach   jeff@spartissf.com   415.555.1529

KENDRA SPENCER

151 WESTCHESTER COURT, SONOMA, CA 95476   707.259.0722   KENDRAJANEDESIGNS@HOTMAIL.COM

EXPERIENCE

Senior Graphic Designer, Silverado Estates, St. Helena, CA
July 2001–Present
- Acted as sole graphic designer for all Silverado Estates wineries
- Create countless original and creative POS campaigns, including backcards, neckers, shelftalkers, etc.
- Designed and illustrated the new Woodriver Vineyard Shiraz logo
- Redesigned Blacksmith Winery County Series packaging to meet new marketing objectives
- Updated and expanded the Silverado Estates portfolio to accommodate it's three new wineries
- Assisted in several indoor and outdoor photoshoots
- Produced high-quality quicksheets under tight deadlines
- Assisted in establishing and updating Brand Standard sheets for each estate
- Oversaw and managed all advertisements and event collateral for three Visitor Centers

Creative Manager/Designer, Olive Advertising, Larkspur, CA
February 1999–June 2001
- Designed logos, stationery, ads, and signs for numerous clients across the United States
- Hand-Illustrated images for logos
- Oversaw all aspects of design from concept to finalization to printing for our departments
- Trained new graphic designers on all aspects of their job
- Wrote and gave performance reviews for graphic designers
- Initiated quarterly creative meetings and departmental meetings as needed
- Interacted with clients daily on design feedback and marketing strategies
- Worked with printers and sign vendors on a regular basis
- Proofed the stationery proofs from the printer

Temporary Production Artist, Timemark Corporate Advertising, Livermore, CA
November 1998–February 1999
- Designed 4-color and b/w advertisements for Timemark's Eastern and Seattle divisions
- Communicated with people across the nation on design and advertising ideas
- Learned to work in a very deadline-oriented environment
- Organized files throughout dozens of nationwide servers

Temporary Designer/Illustrator, HealthServ Industries, Livermore, CA
Summer 1998

Assistant Graphic Designer, City of Martinez, Martinez, CA
Summers & Winter Breaks 1996–1998

EDUCATION   Bachelor of Arts, Fine & Applied Arts, University of Oregon, June 1998

**INTERNATIONAL
EDUCATION**   Instituto d'Arte, Lorenzo de Medici, Florence, Italy, January 1997–April 1997

PROGRAMS   Quark, Illustrator, Photoshop, Microsoft Office

**PERSONAL
STRENGTHS**   Positive attitude, open to new ideas, personable, detail oriented, responsible, organized

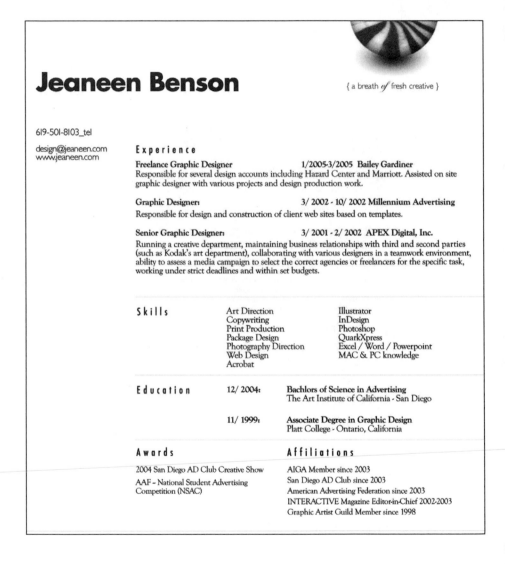

Jeaneen Benson

{ a breath *of* fresh creative }

619-501-8103_tel

design@jeaneen.com
www.jeaneen.com

Experience

Freelance Graphic Designer   1/2005-3/2005 Bailey Gardiner
Responsible for several design accounts including Hazard Center and Marriott. Assisted on site graphic designer with various projects and design production work.

Graphic Designer: 3/ 2002 - 10/ 2002 Millennium Advertising
Responsible for design and construction of client web sites based on templates.

Senior Graphic Designer: 3/ 2001 - 2/ 2002 APEX Digital, Inc.
Running a creative department, maintaining business relationships with third and second parties (such as Kodak's art department), collaborating with various designers in a teamwork environment, ability to assess a media campaign to select the correct agencies or freelancers for the specific task, working under strict deadlines and within set budgets.

Skills

Art Direction	Illustrator
Copywriting	InDesign
Print Production	Photoshop
Package Design	QuarkXpress
Photography Direction	Excel / Word / Powerpoint
Web Design	MAC & PC knowledge
Acrobat	

Education

12/ 2004:   **Bachlors of Science in Advertising**
The Art Institute of California - San Diego

11/ 1999:   **Associate Degree in Graphic Design**
Platt College - Ontario, California

Awards

2004 San Diego AD Club Creative Show

AAF – National Student Advertising
Competition (NSAC)

Affiliations

AIGA Member since 2003
San Diego AD Club since 2003
American Advertising Federation since 2003
INTERACTIVE Magazine Editor-in-Chief 2002-2003
Graphic Artist Guild Member since 1998

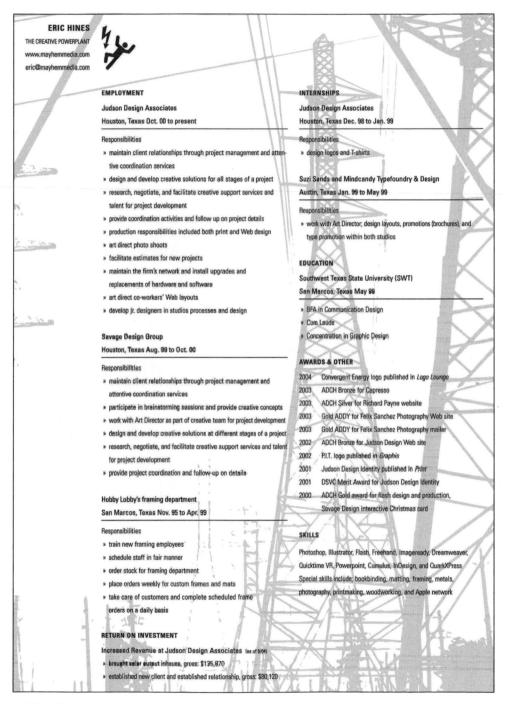

ERIC HINES
THE CREATIVE POWERPLANT
www.mayhemmedia.com
eric@mayhemmedia.com

EMPLOYMENT

Judson Design Associates
Houston, Texas Oct. 00 to present

Responsibilities

» maintain client relationships through project management and attentive coordination services
» design and develop creative solutions for all stages of a project
» research, negotiate, and facilitate creative support services and
   talent for project development
» provide coordination activities and follow up on project details
» production responsibilities included both print and Web design
» art direct photo shoots
» facilitate estimates for new projects
» maintain the firm's network and install upgrades and
   replacements of hardware and software
» art direct co-workers' Web layouts
» develop jr. designers in studios processes and design

Savage Design Group
Houston, Texas Aug. 99 to Oct. 00

Responsibilities

» maintain client relationships through project management and
   attentive coordination services
» participate in brainstorming sessions and provide creative concepts
» work with Art Director as part of creative team for project development
» design and develop creative solutions at different stages of a project
» research, negotiate, and facilitate creative support services and talent
   for project development
» provide project coordination and follow-up on details

Hobby Lobby's framing department
San Marcos, Texas Nov. 95 to Apr. 99

Responsibilities

» train new framing employees
» schedule staff in fair manner
» order stock for framing department
» place orders weekly for custom frames and mats
» take care of customers and complete scheduled frame
   orders on a daily basis

RETURN ON INVESTMENT

Increased Revenue at Judson Design Associates (as of 6/04)
» brought color output inhouse, gross: $135,870
» established new client and established relationship, gross: $80,120

INTERNSHIPS

Judson Design Associates
Houston, Texas Dec. 98 to Jan. 99

Responsibilities

» design logos and T-shirts

Suzi Sands and Mindcandy Typefoundry & Design
Austin, Texas Jan. 99 to May 99

Responsibilities

» work with Art Director; design layouts, promotions (brochures), and
   type promotion within both studios

EDUCATION

Southwest Texas State University (SWT)
San Marcos, Texas May 99

» BFA in Communication Design
» Cum Laude
» Concentration in Graphic Design

AWARDS & OTHER

2004	Convergent Energy logo published in *Logo Lounge*
2003	ADCH Bronze for Capresso
2003	ADCH Silver for Richard Payne website
2003	Gold ADDY for Felix Sanchez Photography Web site
2003	Gold ADDY for Felix Sanchez Photography mailer
2002	ADCH Bronze for Judson Design Web site
2002	P.I.T. logo published in *Graphis*
2001	Judson Design Identity published in *Print*
2001	DSVC Merit Award for Judson Design Identity
2000	ADCH Gold award for flash design and production,
Savage Design interactive Christmas card

SKILLS

Photoshop, Illustrator, Flash, Freehand, Imageready, Dreamweaver,
Quicktime VR, Powerpoint, Cumulus, InDesign, and QuarkXPress
Special skills include; bookbinding, matting, framing, metals,
photography, printmaking, woodworking, and Apple network

Note: The image in the background of this résumé is a watermark when it is printed.

Robert Wees
www.hellorobert.net
GRAPHIC DESIGNER

503+5153729
ROBERT@HELLOROBERT.NET

O

Collaborate. Communicate. Create unique,
intelligent, thought-driven design solutions.

E

Central Washington University, Ellensburg, WA;
Bachelor of Fine Arts in Graphic Design, Advertising Minor.

S

Highly imaginative and technical skills in illustration and typography;

Knowledge of InDesign, Quark, Illustrator, Freehand, Photoshop,
ImageReady, Flash, and Dreamweaver;

Expert user of em-dashes and semicolons.

W

STROMSAND DESIGN, Intern Summer 2003;
Completed twelve-week cooperative learning experience.

CWU PHOTO LAB, Teacher's Assistant 2001–2003;
Assisted photo students in darkroom. Managed darkroom equipment
and chemistry levels. Shot, organized, labeled, and maintained slide
collection. Created lab signage promoting health and safety procedures.

CWU SCHOLARSHIP CENTRAL, Graphic Designer 2000–2002;
Designed and distributed over 100 scholarship posters each academic
year. Created informational brochures with scholarship and financial
budgeting tips. Developed in-office signage facilitating self-guided
scholarship searches. Designed new scholarship web site.

V

PITUITARY HEALTH NETWORK, Lead Designer;
Designed identity system, collateral, and web site for the January
2003 joint press conference with the American Medical Association
(AMA). Art directed a PSA campaign promoting pituitary awareness
and presented it to the national Ad Council in New York City.

CENTRAL JAZZ FESTIVAL, Graphic Designer;
Developed a brand identity system for the CWU band and choral jazz
festival, including logo, brochures, applications, awards, signage, and
festival program. Designed informational vocal jazz web site.

H

Top three winner – 2003 AIGA-Seattle Trapeze Awards, 11th annual
senior portfolio competition.

Outstanding Achievement Award – 2004 HOW Design Self-Promotion
annual, student entry.

215 Thistreet
Anyplace, MA 55555
303-555-2444
address@email.com

Michael Jefferson

Education	***BFA Computer Graphics*** Pratt Institute - Brooklyn, NY
Experience	***Composition Operator*** (10/04 - Present) Aperion – Atown, MA • Maintain visual consistency between pages in all client documents • Prepare files for printing • Position requires meticulous attention to detail to ensure that all documents are printed correctly • Earned several bonuses for exemplary performance in the first three months of employment ***Graphic Designer*** (06/00 – 05/04) Apex Solutions – Atown, MA • Acted as head designer for the Rapid Operations Communications Group • Designed graphics and layouts for brochures, posters, folders, corporate identities, stationary, packages, and Web sites • Established brand identity for several organizations • Maintained brand identity throughout all designs • Prepared files for printing • Managed numerous projects under tight schedules • Involved heavy client interaction • Earned several bonuses for exemplary performance
Digital Skills	***Proficient with:*** • Adobe Photoshop • Maya • Macromedia Dreamweaver • Adobe Illustrator • HTML • MS Office Suite • PC and Mac Platforms ***Working knowledge of:*** • Macromedia Flash • Adobe Premiere • Adobe After Effects • Quark Xpress
Work Samples	Work can be viewed @ http://mysite.com/michael

THANK YOUS

Thanks to all the nice people who agreed to help me make this project a reality. There are a lot of good, generous people out there, though they may seem hard to find at times. Thank you to the staff at Allworth Press for giving me a contract and printing this book. I would also like to thank all the jerks who said they wouldn't help, especially the ones that who a lot of curse words, the people who doubted me, the publishers that rejected me, and the people who said they would contribute to this and then kept me waiting while they did nothing. All that negativity and frustration inspired me to get it finished even faster. Anything is possible if you want it bad enough.

INDEX

skills
  diversification of, 37
  for running businesses, 145, 147, 151, 154–155, 158, 161–162
  temp agencies and, 131
skills test, 48, 99
Small Business Association (SBA), 149
snail mail. *See* regular mail
social change, 161
soul, theft of, 141
spelling, 45, 118
Spokas, Amy, 6–9
  early experiences with art of, 6
  inspiration of, 6
  on interviews, 7, 8
  on job listings, 6, 7
  on research, 8
  on resumes, 8
  unemployment period of, 6
on work samples, 7–8
staff for businesses, 167
standing out. *See* being noticed
Star Wars: The Phantom Menace, ix
stationary, 3. *See also* letterhead
strategies, 35–38
studio work, 7, 37

talent
  education v., 36
  employers on, 54
tax issues, businesses and, 166
telecommunications, 30
telecommuting, xi
temp agencies, 31–32. *See also* Gezelle, Adam; placement agencies
  applying to, 47–48
  assignation by, 102, 103
  benefits of, 98–99
  business owners on, 152
  downtime at, 105

e-mail and, 99
employed graphic designers on, 17–18
employers on, 68–69
interviews at, 102–103, 131–132
job applications for, 99, 132
research and, 104
resumes for, 100, 132
screening processes of, 99
skills for, 131
skills tests of, 99
web sites for, 99
web sites of, 27
work experience and, 100
work samples for, 47, 100–101
temporary placement. *See also* placement agencies; temp agencies
direct hire v., 102–103
temp-to-hire, 133. *See also* blind temp to perm
thank-you letter, 89, 117–119, 126–127, 129
  interviews and, 119
  letterhead for, 118
  regular mail and, 119
Time, 82
Torok, Katie, 146–150. *See also* business owners; businesses
  early experiences with art of, 146–147
  inspiration of, 146–147
trial period, 133
Trump, Donald, xiii
Tull, David, 92–98
  on appearance, 96–97
  on cover letters, 95–96
  early experiences with art of, 92
  on entry level jobs, 94
  on freelance work, 97
  inspiration of, 92
  on internships, 94
  on interviews, 96
  on job descriptions, 93
  on job listings, 92–93

Books from Allworth Press

Allworth Press is an imprint of Allworth Communications, Inc. Selected titles are listed below.

Careers by Design: A Business Guide for Graphic Designers, Third Edition
by Roz Goldfarb (paperback, 6 × 9, 240 pages, $19.95)

Starting Your Career as a Freelance Illustrator or Graphic Designer
by Michael Fleishman (paperback, 6 × 9, 256 pages, $19.95)

How to Grow as a Graphic Designer
by Catharine Fishel (paperback, 6 × 9, 224 pages, $19.95)

The Elements of Graphic Design: Space, Unity, Page Architecture, and Type
by Alex W. White (paperback, 6 1/8 × 9 1/4, 160 pages, $24.95)

Thinking in Type: The Practical Philosophy of Typography
by Alex W. White (paperback, 6 × 9, 224 pages, $24.95)

The Graphic Designer's and Illustrator's Guide to Marketing and Promotion
by Maria Piscopo (paperback, 6 × 9, 224 pages, $19.95)

The Graphic Designer's Guide to Pricing, Estimating, and Budgeting
by Theo Stephan Williams (paperback, 6 3/4 × 9 7/8, 208 pages, $19.95)

Inside the Business of Graphic Design: 60 Leaders Share Their Secrets of Success
by Catharine Fishel (paperback, 6 × 9, 288 pages, $19.95)

Communication Design: Principles, Methods, and Practice
by Jorge Frascara (paperback, 6 × 9, 240 pages, $24.95)

Editing by Design, Third Edition
by Jan V. White (paperback, 8 1/2 × 11, 256 pages, $29.95)

Graphic Idea Notebook: A Treasury of Solutions to Visual Problems, Third Edition
by Jan White (paperback, 8 1/2 × 11, 176 pages, $24.95)

Business and Legal Forms for Graphic Designers, Third Edition
by Tad Crawford and Eva Doman Bruck (paperback, includes CD-ROM, 8 1/2 × 11, 160 pages, $29.95)

Please write to request our free catalog. To order by credit card, call 1-800-491-2808 or send a check or money order to Allworth Press, 10 East 23rd Street, Suite 510, New York, NY 10010. Include $5 for shipping and handling for the first book ordered and $1 for each additional book. Ten dollars plus $1 for each additional book if ordering from Canada. New York State residents must add sales tax.

To see our complete catalog on the World Wide Web, or to order online, you can find us at *www.allworth.com*.